Seeking Paganism
In Search of New Meanings

by
Teresa and Howard Moorey

www.capallbann.co.uk

Seeking Pagan Gods
In Search of New Meanings

©Copyright Teresa and Howard Moorey 2005

ISBN 186163 204 5

ALL RIGHTS RESERVED

No part of this publication may be reproduced, stored in a retrieval system or transmitted in any form or by any means, electronic, mechanical, photocopying, scanning, recording or otherwise without the prior written permission of the author and the publisher.

Cover design by Paul Mason

Published by:

Capall Bann Publishing
Auton Farm
Milverton
Somerset
TA4 1NE

To our forefathers and our sons

Acknowledgments

Our grateful thanks are due to the following, for contributing suggestions for this book: Graham Boston, publisher and astrologer, from Cheltenham; Patrick Corbett, occupational therapist in mental health; Paul Duncan, Brighton bookshop proprietor; Nathan Hatley; Peter Pannet, social worker; James Hunt, personal development trainer with business background - and to others, who wish to remain anonymous.

Howard would also like to acknowledge the authors Janet and Colin Bord and John and Caitlin Mathews for their work, which has been an inspiration for his personal quest.

Also by teresa Moorey, published by Capall Bann:

Wheel of the Year (with Jane Brideson)
The Moon and You
A Basic Guide To Earth Mysteries
The Magic and Mystery of Trees
Experiencing the Green Man (with Rob Hardy)
Astrology For Lovers
Faeries and Nature Spirits

Contents

Chapter 1 In Search of New Meanings	1
Ideas About God	2
Patriarchy	3
The Path of the Seeker	6
Archetypes	7
Homosexuality	7
Parsifal and the Grail	8
Chapter 2 Attuning to Cycles	12
Men and Cyclicity	13
Sexuality	14
Moon Man	16
The Gifts of the Moon	19
Moon Tales	20
Thoth, the Moon God	20
The Yearly Cycle	23
Father, King, Son, Lover - The Seasonal Story	23
Applying the Ideas	26
Oak King and Holly King	27
Gawain and the Green Knight	30
Gwynn Ap Nudd and Gwythyr	31
Osiris and Set	33
Moon Man	34
The Seasonal Cycle	35
Chapter 3 Gods of Wood and Wild	36
The Green Man	39
The Horned God	40
Pan the Goat Foot God	43
Iron John	45
Chapter 4 Hunter, Warrior, Hero	53
Popular Heroes	54
Achievement, Conquest, Campaign	55
Historical Perspective	55
Effects on the Male Psyche	57
Personal Perspectives	58
Homophobia	60
Heroic Images	62
The Hero's Descent	64
Orpheus and Eurydice	64
Commentary	68

i

Don't give a sword to a man who can't dance	68
	68
Ways Forward	68
Cuchulain's Last Battle	71
Chapter 5 Reclaiming Roots and valuing the feminine	74
Sadism In The Male Psyche	75
Historical Comments	77
Masculine and Feminine	78
The Value of the Feminine For Men	81
The Goddess	84
The Ancient Great Mother	85
The Feminine as First	86
The Great Mother as Androgyne	87
The Tower	89
Chapter 6 Other Models	95
The Trickster	95
Fionn Mac Cumhal	96
Loki	97
The Sacred Fool	99
The Magician	100
The Lord of the Dance	100
Shiva	101
The Guardian	102
The Lover	102
Puer and Senex	103
Chapter 7 Final Thoughts	107
Balance	107
Empathy	108
Inanna, Ereshkigal and Enki	108
Initiation	109
The Father	111
Water Jar Boy	112
Commentary	113
Role Models	113
Belief Systems	114
Joblessness	115
Being a Partner	116
Further Reading and Resources	119
Further Reading	119
Resources	120

Chapter 1

In Search of New Meanings

*... come, my friends,
Tis not too late to seek a newer world
... to sail beyond the sunset and the baths
of all the western stars ...*

Alfred Lord Tennyson, *Ulysses*

Currently, many men are conscious of dilemmas, both in their sense of their own identity and in their roles in work and in relationships. It is no longer acceptable to be masterful, dominant and aggressive, but neither is it okay to be a 'wimp'. Male prerogatives are eroded - there are no more jobs for life and fewer and fewer 'jobs for the boys'. Indeed, there are fewer jobs in general, and for those that are available men often have to compete with women - it can be hard for them to accept that they sometimes lose. This is not to say that many men do not accept a female boss gracefully, for lots do. However, what does a man do if he has no job? Men who have hitherto identified themselves with their occupation and status are left with questions. Are there new ways of defining what it means to be a man? Might we find clues to this in our ancient traditions? How might men relate to women? And what about the spiritual dimension? The sense of fulfilment and purpose is receding from the lives of many men.

Ideas About God

And what about God, or gods? Our ideas about such matters are changing, along with so many erstwhile cultural constants. Once upon a time there was belief, atheism or agnosticism - you chose your standpoint, and there was little room to manoeuvre. Most people chose to believe - indeed, to admit to anything else, in some periods in history, was mighty dangerous. Creeds were preordained, based on revelations literally engraved on stone tablets, back in some more graphic, formative era, when the mythical and the revelationary were commonplace. Not that we are really supposed to use the word 'myth' for what was then received was taken as the literal and binding truth. This 'truth' was hierarchical, often punitive, forbidding the pursuit of personal enlightenment, and demanded obedience to the 'word'. Of course, it was patriarchal. God was in His Heaven and all was right in a world where men were naturally on top. Spiritual status quo had arrived, and the faithful had only to do what they were told to be 'saved'. The Age of the Prophets (who were almost always male) belonged to distant history, but their dogmas endured.

Much has been written in recent years about the drawbacks of this approach; how the de-souling of matter and the separation of deity from the material world has left us with so many problems, socially and ecologically; how the denigration of the Feminine has impoverished our culture and our inner selves; how the separation of 'good' and 'evil' has estranged us from parts of ourselves and caused us so much in the way of conceptual conundrums, paranoia, confusion and agonies of conscience. Seekers in their droves are now exploring new ways of being, thinking and feeling, perceiving and reacting. Many are actively pursuing their own forms of enlightenment, and new approaches to spirituality are regularly appearing. Each person may be his or her own 'prophet'.

Considerable numbers of men have welcomed these new ideas warmly, and with relief. Now some of the old structures that have imprisoned them can crumble - such as 'big boys don't cry', 'a man should be master of the house', etc. Men feel freed to be sensitive, not always to take the lead, and many find solace in the fact they no longer always have to appear fearless and aggressive and that sexuality is being liberated from their dominance (and so they are more free to explore other dimensions to their sexuality). There is much to recommend the fact that the whole ethos of war is being questioned and that fresh roles may be open to them. These may be such as house-husband, counsellor, supporter, or less defined ways of being that incorporate a sense of the wild, free and instinctual. However, some may wonder what has happened to the old ideas of heroism, strength, achievement, conquest. Perhaps there are more questions than answers. What may it now mean to be a man?

Patriarchy

Patriarchy means 'rule by the fathers'. One of its functions was to protect paternity, so the male bloodline can remain intact. This still manifests in inheritance laws, where it is taken for granted that the eldest son will inherit property and title, carrying on 'the name'. Resources in society are managed in this way, placing a great deal of power, financial and otherwise, in the hands of men by virtue of birth. In

England a seat in the House of Lords is still acquired thus; girls do not inherit. Basically patriarchy means that everything is owned by men, from spiritual, economic, social and political power through land, property, wealth, even to the bodies of women themselves. Loud voices are raised for 'equality' but in practice change is very slow. The patriarchal mind-set infiltrates everything, without us realising, down even to such words as 'mankind' and the fact that 'he' is used where gender is unspecific - God especially is 'He'. Some say this doesn't matter - the more evolved of us know the Almighty is a spirit and quite above gender. Yet our unconscious minds hear 'he' every time. And the spirit behind patriarchy is even more extensive, for it is the basis for a hierarchical society, based on logical constructs and oriented to achievement, increase, campaign and conquest, ever onward and upward.

Patriarchy means that men and 'masculine' values dominate. These values tend to be authoritarian, monotheistic and often warlike. Thinking is valued over feeling, the intuitive and non-rational are demonised, and judgmental 'black and white' overtones predominate. This attitude is so persuasive that it is hardly questioned. The detrimental effects upon women are now being identified, in some quarters. However, patriarchy is hardly a friend to men either, for it forces them into roles that may be aggressive, authoritarian, competitive and withholding, while condemning many men to positions of 'inferiority' if they do not, or will not, measure up to expectations.

Let us be quite clear about one thing - there have been benefits from the patriarchal approach. Arising initially from the development of a consciousness of the individuality of each person - ego consciousness - patriarchy has tried to give space, at least in some areas, for the human spirit to advance. Having an incisive and masterful approach to the material world, patriarchy has given us many of the comforts of modern life. Without something we may loosely call 'patriarchal' this book could not be produced, and there are many things that could perhaps be regarded as based on a 'masculine' approach that are effectual, helpful and progressive.

However, feeling is growing that this has gone far enough, and the system is being reviewed spiritually and practically. Let us start with the spiritual.

At the top of the hierarchy is usually a God - no in-dwelling spirit but an external creator-overseer. As His delegates upon Earth, men have been given the job of subduing the natural world. This has led, insidiously at first and now at a speed of breakneck destructiveness, to exploitation and grave damage to the ecosystem. The very deeply ingrained mindset of external Father-God doesn't leave much room for true identification with Nature, or respect and value for plants and animals. Sometimes, in its quest for dominance, it leaves scant room for commonsense. Many people feel that the de-souling of Nature has been the principal drawback of the last 2,000 years.

In addition, the affinity of the patriarchal approach to logical systems and clear distinctions has led to some unfortunate 'splits' in our perceptions. These have been weighted by the fact that God, at the top of the tree, needs to be seen as wholly positive, creative and 'good'. So we are left with polarisation - God/devil, good/evil, light/dark, man/woman. The irresistible temptation is to group undesirables together, in order that the foe can be clearly defined for the 'righteous warrior' to fight. Patriarchy loves a good fight against what it may define as 'evil' forces, because then many people (on the right side, of course) can feel good about themselves and this strengthens the system. Sadly, however, the net result is that we become alienated from parts of ourselves. Women have tended to be wrapped up with 'the world, the flesh and the devil' and into the package have been thrown men's passions, emotional needs, spontaneous impulses and sensitivity. The knots are tight and strangling.

On the material level, a patriarchal approach has brought death and suffering to many. Seeking 'power over' rather than 'power to' or 'power within' it has repressed sensitivity and the ability to relate. It has given rise in part to suspicion and competition between man and man. 'May the best man win' is a well-known phrase, but it means most people lose. In the end the only ones who 'gain' are the commanders, emperors, presidents and those at the top of the tree - and we may doubt whether, in the privacy of their souls, they feel fulfiled. Current hierarchical structures cause young men to suspect the old, as Robert Bly explores in Iron John (see Further Reading). Fathers are separated from sons in bastions of learning, industry or government, and what they do becomes more difficult to understand, or to trust. And of course it is the old men who send the young men out to die. Sam Keen (see Further Reading) has these words:

> Our bodies are violated, we are regularly slaughtered and mutilated, and if we survive battle we bear the burden of blood-guilt ... I f we are to honour as well as be critical o f manhood we need to remember that most men went to war, shed blood and sacrificed their lives with the conviction that it was the only way to defend those whom they loved ...

In these pages it is our intention to honour manhood, to look for some new openings and to seek inspiration in the mythical.

The Path of the Seeker

At present there can be no definite answers - and perhaps, in any case, the era of 'definite answers' is past. However, we can try to define some of the questions, discern possible paths and perhaps foster a positive attitude that encourages expectation, adventure and the exploration of potential, rather than the confusion and depression that dogs some men. We can look at the patterns of some well-known myths, and seek for clues and inspiration, and we can examine some of the old role models and epithets to see if they can be revamped, and find new relevance. The spiritual orientation of this book is basically 'pagan' in that we honour Nature and regard religion as being about what you do and feel, about what expands and vitalises you, not about dogma, and we use myths to illustrate points and to bring to life psychological motifs, in the knowledge that no good myth can ever be explained or encompassed fully. First and foremost, a myth is a good story.

Archetypes

Later on we speak about 'archetypes' in some sections. The psychotherapist C. G. Jung said that archetypes exist in the collective unconscious of mankind. They are like a collective instinct, a universal model. Loosely, the word is also used for a collective image or symbol. The idea of the 'anima' or soul, the 'internal feminine' within each man is held to be archetypal - although it must be remembered that Jung's theories are not rigid and are being developed by modern Jungians. Myths are 'archetypal' for they strike a chord in us that can be common to many people, often of different cultures, and their symbolism is vivid and powerful, and psychologically meaningful. We shall be using myths to illustrate and enliven themes. Hopefully you will find them inspiring and interesting.

Homosexuality

Patriarchy does not smile upon homosexuality. One of the origins of the unease with gays may be that gay men are less likely to father children and continue the 'family name'. Traditionally this may have posed problems regarding inheritance. However, homosexuality is treated with suspicion because it blurs distinctions, creates love and closeness between men instead of competition and makes it harder to define what it means to 'be a man'. Homosexuality may be seen in some quarters as a threat to the system. In respect of the issues explored in this book, we found little difference between gays and straights - men generally seem to struggle with similar problems. Several of our contributors are gay - gay men have often been forced to examine their inner selves more closely than straights and so may be rather more self-aware. However, straight men are no less perplexed in general, as to their roles in today's world.

We are ploughing furrows and sowing seeds in the knowledge that men have suffered, are curious and searching. It is important that we all move away from blame or criticism and find fresh perspectives, so men may begin to find themselves in a spirit of love and wholeness.

Parsifal and the Grail

The story of Parsifal and the Grail is told in several different fashions, but the point of the tale rests upon the asking of an important question.

Young Parsifal had remained close to his widowed mother, caring for her, chopping wood and generally helping with domestic tasks. Wishing to shelter her only son, his mother told him nothing of the glories of knighthood, but one day the young man spotted a troupe of gallant knights passing through the wood, and he determined to go to Arthur's court, to seek his fortune.

Parsifal encountered many adventures, as knights do, until one day he decided to return to visit his mother. However, on his way he met a fisherman who directed him to his castle - a strange and deserted place, set in the midst of a wilderness and next to a dank and putrid lake. Mist shrouded the turrets and a brooding silence hung in the air, but Parsifal continued on his way across the drawbridge. Entering the castle he found a hall decked with shabby and decaying splendour. On a couch there rested an old king, crippled by a festering wound in the groin.

As Parsifal stood, wondering, a marvellous and silent procession took place before his eyes. A squire came by with a bleeding lance followed by two other squires carrying candlesticks. Then came a damsel with the cup of the Grail, held high in her arms, and another damsel, with a plate. All these things Parsifal saw, but said nothing. A great weariness came over him and he lay down on the floor and went to sleep. The next morning Parsifal was woken by an ominous rumble. As his chilled and stiffened limbs came back to life, he realised that the castle roof had disappeared and the walls were crumbling fast around him. Reaching for his sword he saw that too was in fragments. Dragging himself to his feet he ran for the drawbridge amidst falling stones, narrowly escaping with his life.

Many years later and now older and wiser, the knight again finds himself in the same spot, and again he crosses the drawbridge of the castle, that is restored to the condition in which he first found it.

Once more he sees the Fisher King lying wounded and once more the strange procession passes before his eyes. But this time Parsifal finds his voice. What ails thee, my brother?' he asks of the King. Turning to the maidens he asks 'What is the Grail? - whom does it serve?'

At this point the Fisher King arises from his sick bed, magically healed. Parsifal discovers that he is the Fisher King's nephew and heir. The barren land is restored to life and health and the people rejoice. As in all the best stories we may assume that everyone lives happily ever after!

Commentary

There are may meanings to this symbolically rich tale. The Fisher King, wounded in the groin, is infertile because he has become estranged from his source. He merely fishes in his polluted lake, instead of being able to immerse himself in the waters and make contact with his own depths. The Sacred Marriage of the King with the land cannot take place, for he is impotent, due to his wound. All is sterile, barren and useless. The bloodied lances continue the image of lost potency.

The Grail, as a symbol of wholeness, is there to heal him. Presumably because of this he does not die. but until the right question can be asked, no proper connection can be made and no solution found.

As with most myths, the story can be an allegory of what happens inside each person, or what happens in the world at large. Many of us are wounded, separated from instinctual source and healthy sexuality.

Many of us dabble in cures as the King fishes, and for many of us healing is within our grasp, but we do not ask the right questions.

For society as a whole the story has the message of the necessity to retrieve the sense of the sacred and valuable in the natural world many people feel the Grail has connections with the Feminine. Certainly it is the cup of life. It contains all the meaning of the totality of the ecosystem, and we need to ask ourselves whom this serves. One answer must be that it serves us.

There is an obsession to find answers, the truth, the absolute, and to solidify it as a graven image that then blocks our way and casts shadows over our path.

How much more important it is to ask the right questions.

Practice

Keep a notebook for recording your thoughts and feelings. You will ': need to use it for the 'Practice' sections in this book. You can start by considering the questions below.

Can you put into words something about your life that perplexes you? There may be many questions, but you may like to formulate one fairly simple question to get you started. Hopefully you will find something in the following pages to bring you closer to an understanding, or reveal a path of enquiry. Most importantly, you may like to ask which areas, concepts, beliefs do you accept without thought or question, making assumptions or simply not noticing that which has always been there? This may be hard to answer - but it may still be worthwhile asking.

Chapter 2

Attuning to Cycles

*We must be still and still moving
Into another intensity
For a further union, a deeper communion
In the end is my beginning*

                         T. S. Eliot *The Four Quartets*

We are all aware of cycles in the natural world. Day follows night, and is followed again by dawn; summer comes after winter, and is succeeded in turn by autumn. In final, glorious flares the leaves blaze and die, fluttering to earth, decaying to mulch; sinking, disappearing, transforming to fertilise roots and arising reborn with the following spring. Seeds go to ground and incubate as winter comes, awaiting the fresh rains and warmth of the new season; animals hide and hibernate, their heartbeats slow and they snuggle in their yearly dreamtime, waiting for the greening, the awakening Sun to come again.

The seasons inspire art and poetry, and we are aware of their beauty. However, to most of us they have lost their meaning. We may respond with complaints or sentiment, or if we are involved — as most of us no longer are — in activities that are seasonal by nature, our approach is pragmatic. But the seasons have much to teach us about wisdom, letting go, hanging on, promoting, receding, changing and developing. The natural cycles of day and night, new Moon to full Moon and back to new again, and the solar cycle from Yuletide to Yuletide have a gentle, insistent message that we can use to sail the tides of our lives.

Learning to 'go with the flow' means we can make best uses of our energies, make less demands on ourselves and generally be more effectual. Most of all, it enables us to feel that soothing, deepening and uplifting sense of being part of something far greater than us, and yet to be uniquely valuable ourselves.

Men and Cyclicity

To women cyclicity is a fact of life, and from puberty onwards their monthly rhythms weld them to a sense of growth and subsiding, potential and contraction, life and death. Men, however, may find they are able to ignore fluctuation. It may have seemed manly to be above such considerations, to be 'master of nature', to carry on regardless with no sense of ebb and flow in one's capabilities. This attitude is now dying among many men, who are all too aware of the value of a sense of cycle and its reality in their lives. In fact, not to cultivate such an awareness can be dangerous, culturally and personally. Nicholas Mann has this to say:

> A woman's archetypal identity is based upon the visible periodicity ... of her body. In her life, her womb, her menstrual cycle and in procreation she is the cosmos. A man's archetypal identity has to be carved out of the

cosmos. He has to impose meaning and structure upon the natural world in acts of will and achievement. This has usually resulted in a preoccupation with external forms and in the making of laws ... The trouble begins when men refuse to die, refuse to go back 'within' and attempt to fix their particular piece of the all as 'it' — as the 'real thing' forever. We have all seen the trouble that degenerate lines of descent ... tyrannical laws, dogmatic institutionalised religions have gotten us into. They are all attempts to fix, establish and institutionalise, in effect, the permanently erect and upward-reaching phallus. Well, we can relax

Men have a yearning to 'relax' but many do not feel able. Their identity (or so they have been told) rests in making their mark, doing, fixing, building, achieving and getting it right and tight for ever and ever, Amen. The toll this takes on the male psyche and the health of the male body can be seen in statistics of divorce and coronary thrombosis. In natural cycles, men can find metaphors and attendant mythology to help them attune to tidal motion, to let go of having to be omnipotent builders of enduring bastions, and to find other sides, other aspects to their nature. This can enrich their inner life and their relationships.

Sexuality

Sexual behaviour has become part of the pattern of pressure to achieve. In this respect men feel they have to be active, dominant, always desirous, potent and ready to 'perform'. This has been nothing less than tragic for many men who are quite unable to be or behave in anything like a manner true to their inner natures, and whose relationships continually founder. Sam Keen, on the basis of the revelations of his Group of Men, gives some of the possible 'headlines' on the, as yet, unclear story about male sexuality:

'We lie a lot about sex, first to ourselves and then to our partners. We are more ambivalent than we appear to be. Tenderhearted, omnipotent studs ... only live in ... fables. Most of us have a difficult time forging a marriage between the heart and the penis. We can't get our tenderness and our potency together. Some of us only want to have sex with a person we love. A lot of us thrive sexually only in marriage. IMPOTENCE IS A NORMAL PART OF OUR SEXUAL CYCLE ...our sexuality has been so formed by our roles as warriors and workers that we do not yet know how to separate our sexuality from ... performance and conquest. We might well ... make a new koan for modern men What was your penis before you were warrior and worker?'

Sensitive men have long departed from the 'Wham, bam, thank you Mam' type of sexual behaviour, but many now find pressures have increased. Not only do men feel they must be constantly ready, they must also hold on to their erection and delay orgasm in order to 'give' a climax to their partner. Consideration is always paramount between loving couples, but responsibility for the orgasm of the other is 'above and beyond the call of duty'. For many men, caught in this bind, lovemaking may become little more than a duty, and their own orgasm may recede to a damp fizzle!

Men who feel they must always be potent - and the word itself is significant, equating male sexuality with power - are condemning themselves to almost certain problems with impotence sooner or later, which they will probably do everything to fight or solve, so dooming themselves to possible chronic dysfunction. Men need to know that it is 'okay' for the penis to be inert, flaccid, unaroused — even in situations where erection would normally be expected. It is worth noting that many men do find their erections do not oblige when in the very situation they might have been expected to rise the proudest — that special date, the long-anticipated time alone with a loved partner. As summer follows winter, so sexual energy will return, but winter cannot be fought or solved, only lived through and valued for itself and its 'inwardness'.

Perhaps the greatest gift lovers may give each other is the gift of their own pleasure. Naturally each couple will experiment and work out ways of loving that delight each of them, but each is 'responsible' for their own orgasm, not that of the partner. Men who are hell-bent on lifting their partner to orgasm after orgasm perhaps can ask themselves what they are trying to prove. In an open, loving relationship no woman will be frustrated, for she will be able to communicate to her partner what she needs and behave herself in a way that will encourage her satisfaction. A man who can relax, who can lose himself in the myriad pleasures his own body can yield him, brings a heartwarming, arousing and rewarding gift to a partner who loves him. Men who can be gentle with themselves as well as their partners, who accept that they are not always 'ready' and who are identified with the waning, shrinking 'inward' side of their nature bring ease and fluidity to their lives and relationships.

Moon Man

One of our contributors sent us a print of a painting by Caspar David Friedrich entitled Two Men Contemplating the Moon. We see the new Moon - the 'old Moon in the arms of the new', a phenomenon caused by earthshine - in the skies by the side of a gnarled tree-trunk. The backs of the men, one leaning his arm on the other's shoulder, are turned towards us - both of the men in the picture, and the onlooker, gaze at the Moon. It is a portrait of masculine comradeship in the face of the eternal and the cyclical.

On their first evening together Howard told Teresa 'I am as cyclical as you'. Howard had observed that his energy, enterprise, concentration and sexual interest fluctuated, reaching a peak at full Moon and receding at new Moon, when he generally found he needed more rest. Being involved in the demanding world of commerce and finance, it was not, and is not, possible to modify activity to any great extent, but Howard found that by honouring his varying requirements as best he could he was able to function better than by trying to go hell for leather at all times. Thus full Moon might be a time to tackle DIY, budget balancing, any other pressing matters that require energy, to take walks and generally to be active and achieving. New Moon, on the other hand, indicates a need for more sleep, to husband energy resources so that the requirements of job and home are covered, and to allow activity to recede, as much as is practical, so that potency can build as the Moon waxes.

The Moon, as well as being a very beautiful and hypnotic companion at night time, can be invaluable in showing a man a path to his own inner cyclicity. Understandably, many men wish to be very private about such matters, but the advantage of knowing one's own 'waxing and waning' can be considerable. Simply observing the Moon and the relation of the phases to one's own life can be a great beginning in contacting hitherto unconscious aspects. We saw in Chapter 1 how the psychologist Carl Jung wrote that men possess an inner feminine side, the 'anima', which is the root of much creative impulse and often influences choice of female partner. Merely observing the Moon on a steady basis, without too much in the way of intellectual input, may put a man in touch with these vital inner springs and relieve him somewhat from eternally seeking them in a real-life woman, who can never wholly embody his dream image or take the place of his own spontaneity and inspiration.

Here are some evocative words from Nathan Hatley about his experience of the Moon:

There was a time once that she meant nothing to me. When she was a feature as real and concrete as a building or natural landmark. She wasn't a stranger, how could she be? We had walked upon her, played amongst her still dust, stuck poles in her claiming her as our own. All this before I had been born. No, she held no mystery, just a beautiful milky stone that nobody wanted anymore.

But that was a time before this, a time when I dwelt in a hard, rational, concrete world. A world of routine, of noise, of traffic, of paper. This was a world measured in time, distance and final demands for payment. A world of blissful ignorance viewed with the predator's eye, a world of hard objects to be negotiated. This world was the world of deep sleep before the dreaming began.

Even as I took my first tentative steps towards the abstract, she remained largely ignored, a picture postcard image viewed from a window. Besides she made me uneasy, a vague fleeting feeling like I was missing something. Then one night my growing energy and awareness feeling particularly strong, I fell in love with her. She was in full Piscean bloom, clear and sharp, leaping from a cloak of nightclouds as if it was her will to catch me unawares. I was transfixed, rooted to the floor, she filled my gaze until nothing, absolutely nothing else mattered. I felt so small, so unimportant, yet so powerfully male, so strong within myself. I had with me my dolholla, and my fingers began tapping a rhythm upon the head of the drum almost of their own accord. The more she held me the stronger I played, as if I wanted to woo her from the very sky and bed her myself. Then just as quickly she discarded me, slipping demurely behind her veil of cloud. And I watched her go. And I never forgot.

Now she is a mystery to me and I wonder about the hold she exerts over the earth. And I wonder about the incredible urge to mate, the unbridled passion and sexual charge that courses through my body when she rises to the peak of her lunar cycle. Finally I wonder why, deep down, I am a little afraid of her?

The Gifts of the Moon

As a representative of cyclicity, the Moon is unequalled. In the early evening rises the waxing crescent, signaling new beginnings, freshness, a surging forth of ideas and enterprise. As the month progresses the Moon rises later, until the full Moon presides over a glowing, magical midnight. This is a period of fulfilment and fruition, and often of high energy. Then, as the waning crescent is slowly lost in the dawn sky, consciousness turns inward, introspection may be indicated, a slowing, deepening, reflective time comes on, before the Moon again waxes.

The Moon represents the intuition, the mysteries that lie below the bright light of consciousness, that is more usually represented by the Sun. Queen of the night time and of the instinctual kingdom that logic cannot penetrate, the Moon is often regarded as feminine, but she has equal riches to bestow upon men. In addition to the link with wordless, enchanted yet natural realms, the Moon is also connected to the development of abstract thought — for the Moon disappears each month for about three days, between old and new. In this way the Moon taught our forebears the principle of holding in the mind an object, while the object itself had disappeared, of expecting and predicting its return, of observing the logic of ebb and flow as well as its symbolic meaning. Although we often see the Moon as feminine, we also speak of the 'man in the Moon' and there have been many Moon gods.

Moon Tales

Some native peoples see the Moon as masculine, calling him 'the husband of the women'. It was believed that the Moon caused pregnancy, and certainly many people see the Moon as linked with women's periods. So a man may see in the Moon a metaphor for his own seeding, generative capacity, and may also observe that this waxes and wanes. As the Moon shines, so a man may be aware of his vital energy, feeling his being and consciousness expanding.

The shape of a hare is often identified in the lunar shadows. A tale tells of the Lord Buddha, who encountered a hare while wandering tired and hungry through the forest. In order to help him the hare instructed the Buddha to build a fire and boil upon it a pot. When the water was boiling the hare leapt into the pot to provide a meal for the Lord, who then showed his magical powers, plucking out the hare and placing him in the Moon, as a place of honour — thus immortalising his spirit of sacrifice. We can note from this the importance of true sacrifice — not, we might stress, the necessity to offer oneself up as sustenance for another, but in sacrifice of the ordinary, everyday self to the deeper self. In other words we may give up what is of no true value, although this may be painful, in order to find what is spiritually important to us. This is a healthy 'letting go' about which the Moon has much to suggest to men.

Thoth, the Moon God

Thoth was one of the Egyptian pantheon, having sprung from primeval Chaos. He was god of wisdom and scientific endeavour, being a very ancient deity from pre-dynastic times. Thoth was a Moon god and a measurer of time. In this we see a combination of the concept of cyclical, rhythmic time and intuitive 'knowing' with linear—logical time and more scientific intelligence for the same wisdom that led Thoth to identify with the Moon also showed him that the lunar calendar does not fit neatly into a year defined by movements of the Sun. Janet and Stewart Farrar (*see further reading*) tell us that this led Thoth to '... devise a cunning solution and thus to distance himself from his own lunar origins; all of which, of course, is a mythologising of mankind's own process of realisation'.

The story happened in this way: Nut, the sky goddess, had married Geb, the Earth, against the wishes of Ra, the Sun god. Ra ordered the air god, Shu, to come between them, and stated that Nut should have no children in any month of the year. But Thoth, concerned with balance, compassion and, we might suppose, the instinctual realms, sympathised with the lovers. Cunningly he played draughts with the Moon, winning a seventy-second part of the Moon's light, and he turned these into five intercalary days that belonged to no month. From this was made a very accurate calendar of 365 days, and Nut was enabled to give birth to Osiris, Horus the Elder, Set, Isis and Nephthys during the 'spare' days. Here we see Thoth as a champion of fairness and balance, which is extended by his marriage to Ma'at, goddess of truth and cosmic order. Together they weighed the souls of the dead against the feather of Ma'at to find out how true the soul had been to destiny.

The figure of Thoth can be an inspiring one to men striving to harmonise their instinctual side with the demands of order, balance and clear thought. Above all, this story about Thoth gives an example of the compassionate use of cunning to bring about creativity.

SAMHAIN · MIDWINTER · IMBOLC · SPRING EQUINOX · BELTANE · MIDSUMMER · LUGHNASADH · AUTUMN EQUINOX ·
31 OCT · 22 DEC · 2 FEB · 21 MAR · 30 APR · 22 JUN · 31 JUL · 21 SEP ·

The Yearly Cycle

While the Moon is often thought of as feminine, equally the Sun is often held to embody the masculine, (although we are aware that there are many solar goddesses) and so the solar rhythms during the year can be a source of inspiration to men. Our contributor, Paul Duncan writes:

> In my personal experience the yearly waxing sun — Oak King, and waning sun — Holly King, describe well the simple lifetime's cycle of a man. Joining with the sun as one is a holy and heartwarming and empowering experience that no man should miss.

Paul feels that it is important to feel empowered and to be able to glory in one's sexuality, as a man, without attacking the waning, destroying aspect of maleness. In this, the yearly cycle is a powerful, pervading symbol.

Father, King, Son, Lover - The Seasonal Story

Many ancient mythologies enshrine the story of the Son/Lover to the Goddess. The spirit of the hunted animal (who is deeply revered as the source of life) and the vegetation god, cut down with the harvest to resurrect next year, is embodied in many gods such as Tammuz (with Ishtar) Attis (with Cybele) Adonis (with Venus) and Oriris (with Isis). In these myths we see the Mother Goddess loving, mating with, conceiving by, consenting in the death of, and bringing back to life, the person of the God. The Goddess is the earth who continually destroys and rebirths living creatures, and the God is that very life, which comes and goes.

The above-mentioned gods are 'sacrificial gods' and sometimes human sacrifice was practised, at various times of the year, in honour of this process. Jesus Christ can be seen as a sacrificial god in line with this ancient tradition. One of our correspondents has these words:

My coming across Jesus as a vegetation deity and fertiliser of mother earth occurred many years ago at the Easter Vigil Service when the priest held aloft the paschal candle ... and dipped it into a 'cauldron' of salt water ...The experience spoke to me of male virility and the essential of unifying with my feminine side which I have come to value and acknowledge in myself and others.

Some people object to this image of the masculine as little more than 'Big Mama's sidekick' and this view is understandable. However, some men find in it a sense of repose. The masculine is here shown as every bit as necessary as the Feminine, for while the Goddess may 'contain' the God, as She is the cycle itself, while He is the one that travels it, yet the God is the manifestation of the Goddess, without whom She would remain unproductive, unmanifest, without vitality. The story of the Goddess and Her Son/Lover has been reclaimed in a variety of ways by modern Nature worshippers (whom we may call pagans). Let us look more closely at how this story unfolds, with relevance to the ancient yearly festivals.

Samhain (pronounced sa-ween) 31 October
This is the old Celtic New Year, for to the Celts darkness was a time of beginnings. A time of story telling and remembering the ancestors, this was also a sad time when harsh decisions had to be made about livestock that needed to be culled and other necessary cutting back, to survive the winter. At this time the God is Underworld deity, King of the Shadows. He resides in the Islands of the Blessed as guardian of mystery. This was a major festival, possibly marked by human sacrifice at one time, later Christianised as 'All Souls'.

Yule
This is the time of the winter solstice, on or around 22 December. Now is the time of the birth of the Sun God anew, from the womb of the Mother. Veneration of this is reflected in

such structures as Newgrange, in Ireland, where the rays of the solstice Sun penetrate deep into earthworks built especially for this. We mark the renewal of life by Christmas trees and Yule logs, and gifts are exchanged in honour of the 'baby Sun'.

Imbolc
This means 'in the belly'. The date for this festival is 2 February, when the life of the God is seen and felt to stir within the land and within the belly of the Goddess. Days grow longer and the first flowers peep out.

Spring Equinox, around 21st of March
Now the fertility of Nature is in full swing and we may visualise the young, vigorous God testing his skills in the woodland. Easter eggs echo themes of birth and awakening.

Beltane 30 April
Along with Samhain this is perhaps the most important of the festivals. To the Celts, who are believed to have had only two seasons, summer began here. The air tingles with excitement. This is the time when the young God meets the Goddess, courts Her and They fall in love and mate on the bright new grass. Beltane is the representation of manhood in full vigour.

Midsummer, around 22 June
Now the Sun and the God are at full strength, but a turning point is reached — for at the hour of greatest light, so light begins to die. In the fulfilment of His ardour the God begins to look inward, to question and wonder. He is making ready for a journey.

Lammas/Lughnasadh (pronounced loo-nu-sah) 31 July
The first of the harvests are gathered and with them the God is 'cut down'. We see this in the idea of the Corn Spirit, John Barleycorn. It was considered unlucky to cut the last of the harvest, and special sheaves were kept as corn dollies, to

retain seeds to be planted next year. Lugh is a Celtic god of light and craftsmanship, while Lammas means 'loaf mass'. The bounty of the harvest and the gift of the God are celebrated in loaves and other produce. Now the God begins His Underworld journey.

Autumn Equinox, around 22 September
A season of hauntings when the veil between this world and Otherworid is thin. The God has departed for other realms and we look within, meditating, contemplating meanings, as the life-force withdraws for the winter. And so to Samhain again.

There are many, many meanings to these seasonal festivals, with lots of appropriate traditional observations. If you are interested in exploring further, you may like to consult *The Wheel of the Year - Myth and Magic Through the Seasons* in this series. For our purposes here, the most important point is the notion of male cyclicity embodied in the journey of the Sun and the saga of the God.

Applying the Ideas
As in the case of all myths, we should not be literal about applying the concepts. The message is that there is a time and a season for all things. Some times are right for beginnings, others are correct for us to commit ourselves with energy and passion, at others it is more appropriate to withdraw, to focus upon our hidden landscapes, in a sense to 'die' in some form, so that new life may emerge.

In following this model you do not have to be exact about the seasons, for the vast majority of men will not feel it is appropriate or desirable to 'withdraw' throughout the winter. Rather this is about getting in touch with our inner need to recede at times that feel right for us. Certainly it is about honouring that part of the masculine psyche that is so important and powerful, but that has been long obscured and neglected — this is the part that needs to explore the mysterious, the destructive, the catabolic as opposed to the anabolic, the breaking down, dismembering aspect, the darkness in which hides the light. Such 'destruction' is not mindless or concerned with negative use of power or conquest - it is about identifying with natural law.

Oak King and Holly King

These are the personifications of the light and the dark aspects of the God that some people prefer to the idea of Son/Lover. The Oak King is king of the waxing year, from Yule to Midsummer, while Holly King reigns from Midsummer to Yule. Stories and rituals picture them battling at Yule and Midsummer. At Yule, Oak King wins, at Midsummer it is Holly's turn, Neither is 'better' than the other, neither reigns eternally, for these are twins and each is an aspect of the other. Holly King and Oak King are aspects also within each individual man. Paul Duncan gives us this litany:

I am the creator and the destroyer
I am the light and the dark
I am the living and the dead
I am the star and the Nova
I am the Spring and the Autumn
I am the young man and elderly gentleman
I am the holy and the evil

So accustomed are we to duality, to 'splitting' terms such as light and dark, good and evil, that such balance may be hard to accept. Without doubt we can see that Nature is composed of creation and destruction, and that both are necessary, and that neither can go on for ever. Here we have the yin and the yang, dark and light, each carrying within it the seed of the

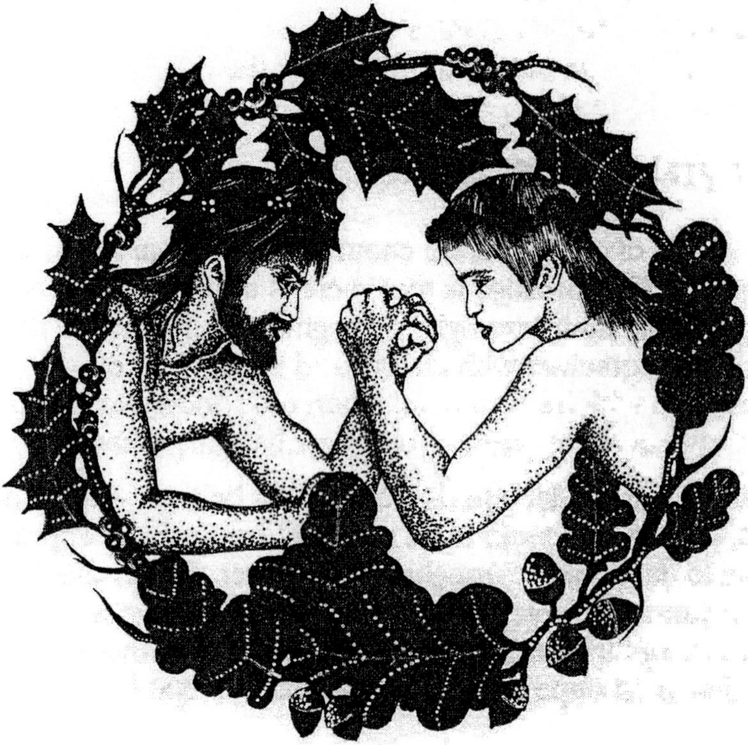

other. Attempts to encompass this conceptually always give rise to conundrums. If good and evil are polarised as in the Christian model, the ever-plaguing dilemma of an 'omnipotent' God who creates the devil, sin and misery, lingers on. If we accept that good and evil are two sides of one coin, then we have also to take on board that there are forces in the universe which are most unpleasant for us, but which are necessary.

Two important points emerge. One is our need to accept parts of our own personalities that we may suppress as undesirable. This is not in order necessarily to indulge them (needless to say, this is not a license to rape and mass murder, although such impulses may well be more a result of 'splitting' than a move away from it). Rather it is in order to know they are there and to welcome them as meaningful aspects of our totality. If more men had the honesty that Nicholas Mann is quoted as expressing, concerning rape, in a later chapter, then more would have true self-control and integration. Our second point is that the above litany has value, not to the conscious mind, that cannot make sense of opposites, but to the unconscious, that understands quite well the meaning of 'the living and the dead the holy and the evil'.

You may celebrate your light and your dark side, your open, bright, sensible and logical side and your closed, dimmed, chaotic and intuitive side, your creative side and your destructive side - you may explore them. The seasons give you permission. The Sun shows you the way.

Gawain and the Green Knight

The motif of Holly King and Oak King appear in many myths. Nicholas Mann calls them Serpent Son and Star Son respectively.

We also meet them in the persons of Gawain and the Green Knight.

The Green Knight turns up at the court of King Arthur one Yuletide, huge and strange, wearing a crown of greenery and holly berries. He challenges any knight to behead him on condition that he can strike the return blow. Sensing the presence of the supernatural, the older knights do not respond. It takes the freshness and valour of young Gawain to take up the challenge.

Gawain swings his sword and the Green Knight's head springs from his body. The court cheers, but their applause dies in their throats. For the Green Knight remains upright, his headless body strides forward, and the severed head lets out a mighty laugh. Bending, the Green Knight retrieves his head and replaces it on his shoulders. Now Gawain must be ready for the return blow the following year.

Like all true knights, Gawain sets out on a quest for the Knight's Green Chapel, where he will presumably meet his death. He stays at the castle of Sir Bertilak, whose beautiful wife tries to seduce him. Gawain, loyal to his host, does not succumb, but he accepts the gift of her girdle, which protects the wearer from death. When he goes forth to meet the Green Knight he sustains only a light wound on the neck. The Green Knight reveals now that he and Sir Bertilak are one and the same. We may wonder if Sir Bertilak's 'wife' is the Goddess, favouring both champions. Light and dark remain in balance. The Green Knight's mystery and the valour of Gawain complement each other; neither can be expressed fully, on its own.

Gwynn Ap Nudd and Gwythyr

Here we have a Welsh myth that centres on the well-known landmark of Glastonbury in Somerset. Gwynn, the Underworld King, leads out the Wild Hunt over the Tor on dark and stormy nights - especially Samhain - as he herds the lost souls of the dead into his realm. Gwynn is said by some to dwell beneath the Tor, the abiding and awe-inspiring spirit of the earth energies that vibrate there. Gwynn loves Creiddylad (the Goddess, of course) and his perpetual rival for her is Gwythyr ap Greidyawl. These two battle at Beltane and Samhain (not at Yule and Midsummer), and Gwynn is banished for the light half of the year, only to ride out again when the cold jaws of winter open and mist creeps from the moors to envelop the Tor.

In later versions, St Michael replaced Gwythyr and vanquishes Gwynn as the dragon - but the older myths are wiser, for the struggle between light and dark goes on. Neither can defeat the other, and neither should, for they are equally valuable and together they bring together cosmic duality.

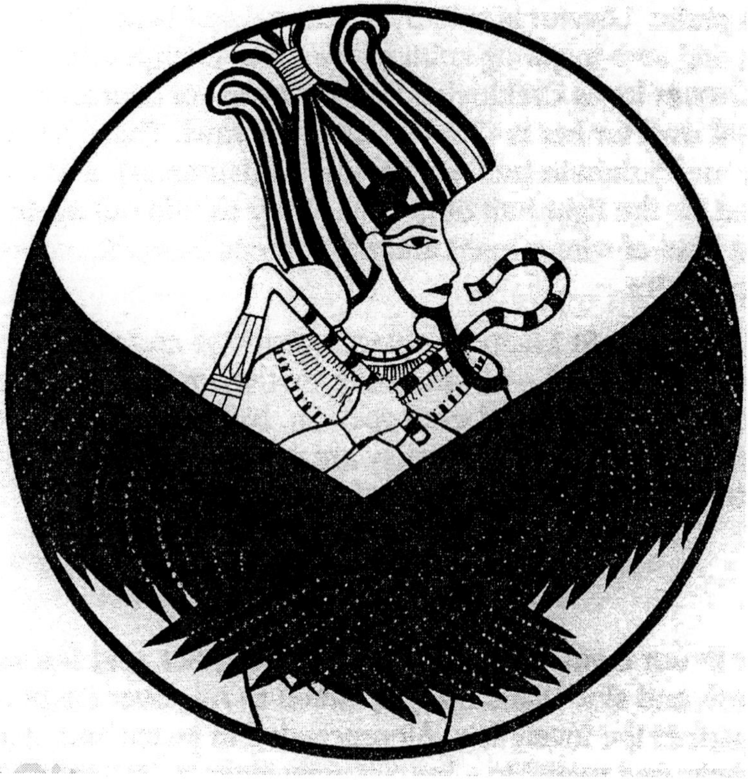

Osiris and Set

We saw in our myth about Thoth that Osiris, Set, and Isis were born from earth and sky. Osiris was appointed to rule over Egypt and had as his partner the lovely Isis. All proceeded in peace and plenty under their wise rulership - but Set grew jealous. Pretending to put on a feast in his brother's honour, he tricked Osiris into getting into a special, jewelled casket. As soon as Osiris was inside, Set and his followers sprang upon it and nailed it down. The coffin, which the magnificent casket now was, floated out to sea and was lost.

Isis, sorrowing and desperate, managed at last to retrieve her husband's body from where it had come to rest in a tamarisk tree. Through magical arts she revived him and conceived their son, Horus the Younger. Set, however, had not finished. Seizing the body of his brother, he hacked it into fourteen pieces and distributed these over the Nile Delta. Isis found each one, trailing through mud and tree-roots to complete her gruesome task. The only piece that could not be found was the phallus of Osiris, so Isis, through magic, made him a replacement.

Osiris was now transmuted. He chose to remain as ruler of Amenti, Land of the Dead, rather than return to Earth. Especially his organ of generation, his phallus, was different, for now it was a product of magic and so able to generate the Otherworldly, the transformative and the magical itself, rather than physical children. Horus, his son, remained alive in the upper world to avenge him against Set.

Here we see the seasonal cycle embodied by Set and Osiris/Horus - for Horus is an alter-ego of his father. Each year Osiris would rise with the Nile, and each year Set came in the presence of drought and the dry desert. Osiris himself is dual, for he is both Father—God and Underworld deity. In

Osiris men may find a model for different aspects and discover their power to self-fertilise, inwardly, with the powers of knowledge, meditation and introspection. Osiris is deposed in the twenty-eighth year of his reign and his body cut into fourteen pieces - both these numbers are linked to the days of the lunar cycle. Osiris is a cyclical deity in truth who can lead the way into the mysteries for men are inspired by him. He is portrayed sitting enthroned, wearing the crown of Upper Egypt and carrying the crook and scourge of royal status.

Practice

Moon Man

Locate the days of new Moon and full Moon on your calendar. Keep a special diary, or construct your own chart on a large sheet of paper, making squares for each day from one new Moon to the next you will need twenty-nine squares (twenty-eight is the approximate number of days it takes for the Moon to return to the same place in the zodiac, which is not the same as lunar phases).

What are the areas of life that are most important to you? Do you need lots of physical energy, or is mental concentration of paramount concern? Enthusiasm, optimism/pessimism, sexual energy, creativity, emotions, 'gut feelings' - any or all of these and more may be important to your life. Decide that you will record how these fluctuate during the month - you may like to colour-code using different pens for sexual, emotional, intellectual and so on. Whatever type of energy is important in your life can be mapped. Do this daily at a preset time, perhaps morning or evening. After a few months - probably three is the minimum, compare notes. It is probable that you will find certain lunar phases are better for certain activities. Do not prejudge. For some, full Moon may be the most active, for some new Moon. You may be a person who 'comes to life' at the dark of the Moon, or full Moon may be your inspiration.

You can discover this only by recording and experimenting. When you have reached a conclusion you can put your discoveries to practical use in your life. In this way your energies find their greatest effect.

The Seasonal Cycle
You may consider your life generally in terms of the seasons - for instance, you may be going through a 'winter' period now, even if the Sun is shining and it's thirty degrees outside! Observing cyclicity is about being true to yourself, being 'with' who and where you are, for your winter can turn to summer in its own time.

Especially you may find it helpful to begin observing the seasonal cycle. Where are you now, in your part of the world, in terms of the seasons? Remember: if you live in the Southern Hemisphere the dates will be rotated and your Midsummer will, of course, fall in December. You may like to start making notes of your thoughts and feelings about the next festival to come. How does it make you feel? What times in your life does it remind you of? What has happened to you before at this season? How would you like to mark it? Are there activities, sports, or creative pursuits that seem appropriate? Is it a time for a new start, a time to consolidate, to think, meditate, break free, be alone, seek company, forge bonds, make an ending, find inspiration? Are there pictures, poems or phrases that spring to mind? Do all you can to identify with the spirit of the time now here, in order to get in touch, in due course, with your own cycles and hidden abilities.

Chapter 3

Gods of Wood and Wild

*In caverns deep the old gods sleep
But the trees still know their Lord
And it's the Pipes of Pan which call the tune
In the twilight of the wood*

Vivienne Crowley, The Pipes of Pan

Most of the enduring structures of society, from high-rises to codified laws, are 'manmade'. This means that not only are they 'unnatural' and synthetic, they are also the product, to a large extent, of the male of our species. The phrase 'it's a man's world' is now strongly challenged, but there is no doubt that it has been, in many respects, a 'man's world'. Men now face many hurdles and many questions. What should be destroyed and what preserved, where are the new models to be found, and how can man, as a sex, reconnect with the world of Nature without losing something that is essential to masculinity? Our contributor, Paul Duncan, speaks of the necessity to '... reinstate man's role with nature as a creative fertilising being rather than just an aggressive destroyer who needs to be tamed'. Nicholas Mann writes:

> While men are the creators of hierarchy, they also have the power to connect with every part o f the cosmos they create and not maintain dualities of which they refuse to recognise half. Men can reconnect the daemonic to the transcendental, heaven to hell, earth to spirit if they so choose.

In other words, men can be spiritual and 'whole' as well as builders and achievers. The author goes on to explain how special sites where 'earth power' is felt strongly, such as the underground chambers of Neolithic mounds, were probably used for male initiation.

> ... This was essentially a process that brought the potentially destructive energies of men into the sacred space - the time of creation - and impressed upon them the sacred template o f the cosmos.

Forms of initiation for men are conspicuous by their absence in our society. Initiation means many things - it means opening out to a deeper and wider consciousness, it means a realisation of the position of oneself in the cosmos and one's true responsibilities therein, it means coming into a sense of power, and it means a realisation of the presence of the numinous, the mysterious - recognising the existence of this and at the same time knowing it can never be controlled. Initiation is a time of body knowledge and spirit knowledge, when one becomes 'plugged in' to a greater force, the current of life and death - and more. For girls, this happens with the start of menstruation, and although this may remain largely unmarked or poorly dealt with, at least it is something. For young men there is nothing whatsoever of any depth.
Without a connection to this sacred current, men are in

danger of becoming inflated, of creating systems that bear no relation, and are destructive to the natural world on which they depend. By the same token, men are cut off from a huge source of potency. A world where men have reconnected to their internal source, where they respect and celebrate the organic and the feral and find a way of blending this with their upward-reaching, constructing impulses - such a world is an exciting vision indeed.

There is a wealth of myth and symbol that men may call on, to reclaim their own, masculine affinity with the world of Nature. These do need developing by modern men in a modern context. A Cheltenham publisher and astrologer, Graham Boston, contributes these comments:

> Myths of ancient Egypt, Sky Gods, The Sacred River, Nature Spirits and Elementals, the Garden of Eden to name but a few - these symbols, myths, call them what you will, have meaning for me. perhaps in part due to their being so opposite of our everyday experience. For me there has to be mystery and a sense of the sacred.

Graham is calling, it seems, for images that can evoke the vivid 'Otherworld' that is closer to our source, that lies beneath and within the day to day, and inspires and empowers it - but that we can so easily miss. He seeks another dimension to experience. Such images seem miles from our concrete-and-clay existence. Here we offer some traditional masculine figures that encompass the sacred and the elemental and may show a path into some form of initiation. albeit internal. These are starting points on which readers may like to expand.

Our contributor James Hunt, also sees the value in these archetypes. By use of movement he seeks to reconnect with such forces as the Wild Man, Sacred Fool and Hero within himself. Many men, including James, are conscious of a strong 'feminine' side within them that is quite well developed. It can be misleading to speak of men as 'left-brained' when their instinctual aspects predominate. For such men, the 'male' aspect may feel quite primitive and basic - for James, cultivating this energy means going deep within to uncover the instinctual. Some gay men may also find this helpful, finding in these images an access to a raw and powerful side.

The Green Man

The Green Man is a fairly recent term that has come to be applied to various images of Nature gods and especially the foliate mask. It is interesting that this face of greenery appears so often in ecclesiastical medieval architecture, and it seems that the masons may have been making a point!

The face of the Green Man is composed of leaves. Leaves issue from his mouth and nose, they sprout, horn-like from his head, leaves form his beard, moustache and eyebrows. However, there is more to the Green Man than a face of leaves. His vitality is huge, irrepressible. He peeps from every hedge and thicket, he leaps in each woodland shadow, and the west wind is his belly-laugh. He delights in the ironic and the mildly absurd, especially when it shows the folly of cerebral systems. In his majestic, impish presence he asserts the primacy of natural law.

The English folk hero, Robin Hood, is a type of Green Man. Living deep in the woods with his band of merry men pouncing upon bejeweled lords and pompous prelates, robbing them of their goods and their dignity - but not their lives, he represents the balancing factor within Nature. Robin Hood is well known for his practice of robbing the rich to give to the poor. He is no respecter of high office or ecclesiastical status - he 'cuts through the crap', redistributing wealth where it is needed. He is a great leveller, and a great reveller, and in him the wisdom of the trees comes to life.

The Green Man exemplifies 'tree power'. As symbols, trees are unparalleled and many cosmologies are based on their ability to connect soil and sky. Their roots twine into the Underworld, their strong trunks inhabit our four-dimensional ordinary world, while their foliage reaches towards the transcendent heavens. There is an enchantment about trees that is impossible to define, and this may be because they possess their own, highly evolved consciousness that stretches into other dimensions. Trees are the 'lungs' of our planet, breathing the breath of life, and they embody the self-sacrifice of the vegetable kingdom, that presents itself for our use yet retains its dignity, even as a log or a dry leaf.

The Green Man is represented mostly as a head. The head was revered by the Celts as the seat of wisdom and eloquence, which they emphasised in the rather doubtful practice of head-hunting! The Green Man is the poetry, the song, the oratory of the trees, rendered in human measure. In the Green Man we see root power, humus, loam and dirt power, the power of the Underworld, the chthonic and the primeval, translated into leafy words. The foliate mask speaks to the heart of man of his source and potential. You may listen to his words simply by looking at his head - no analysis is necessary.

The Horned God

Gods with horns appeared in many guises until the advent of Christianity subverted them as devils - the gods of the old religion became the devils of the new. As horns have been especially demonised, we can look perhaps at the values of the religion that superseded them for hints as to their meaning.

Many of the early churchmen were extremely anti-sex and disdainful of the material world. Women especially were regarded as potentially evil, unless they were kept on a tight rein and humbled. Of course, most Christians today do not take such views, but there seems to be a streak in Christian thinking that regards the earthly as sinful.

To the Horned God, sex is a sacrament and a celebration. He wears his virility on his head, as if power were drawn up from the phallus into a crown of vitality and flagrant animality. There is more here than the urge to copulate, for it is as if sexual energy has awakened all the chakras - energy centres within the body - and burst gloriously through the scalp. Horns mean knowledge of one's generative power and of being part of the cosmic order. They speak of an awakened consciousness that is potent, active, creative and yet deeply identified with the world of Nature.

The horns may be taken to have several specific meanings. Some horns imitate the curve of the Fallopian tubes and as such are an oblique salute to the Goddess. Others are more like the crescent Moon, or the branches of a tree. Horned masks are worn in rituals by contemporary pagans or as part of folk customs, such as the Abbots Bromley Horn Dance, which takes place in early September. At their simplest, horns can be seen as representing fertility, but much deeper significance is also indicated. In Shakespearian times 'wearing the horns' was a description of a man whose wife was unfaithful. It is hard to see the connection, other than the fact the horns signified that the man had no control over the instinctual world, as symbolised by his wife.

However, the instinctual is part of the God. We honour it because it is honourable, not seeking to control it, or be controlled but to celebrate and to be aware.

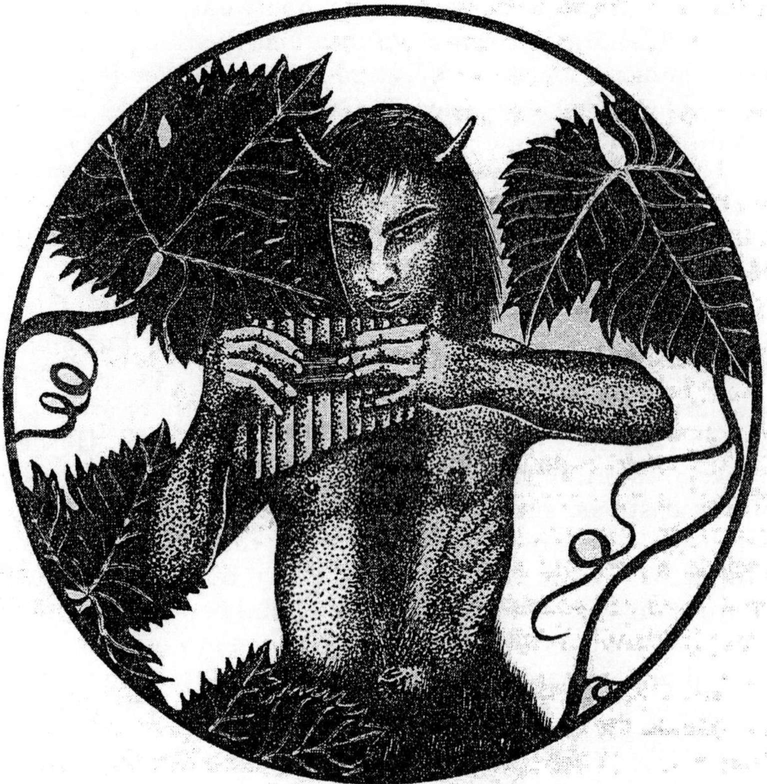

Pan the Goat Foot God

Pan was the god of shepherds and pasture, especially in rustic Arcadia. Some myths speak of him as the son of Hermes, the tickster. However, Pan has the aura of the ancient, the mute forces of Nature that are unfathomable, and may be dangerous. His name means 'all', and 'panic' derives from it. Such is the strange fear that can come upon us when we are alone on hillside or in forest, and we can hear no human sound but our own crazy heartbeat. It is then that Pan is close by. Janet and Stewart Farrar describe him beautifully:

> His physical appearance reflects ... the total spectrum of reality. He had goat's feet, in touch with the earth. His animal legs rose to his fertilising, energising loins. His torso was purely human, culminating in his wise and prophetic head, with its power of creating music. Pan is 'All' indeed.

Pan was known for the strange, wild music that he played on his pipes. This is how he made them. Pan fell in love with the beautiful nymph, Syrinx, but unlike many maidens she evaded him. She was a follower of the maiden-goddess, Artemis, and Pan's hearty sexuality was too much for her. She ran from him, but he followed on his goat's hooves, grinning gleefully. Many women had run from him, but they had made sure they didn't run too fast. Pan was aware that he could pleasure a woman like no other god, not even great Zeus of the many loves.

Syrinx, however, was an exception. Pan couldn't understand why she was running so fast, and he could hear her whimpering and praying on the breeze. He slowed, doubtful now, but still wanting her. How lovely her fair hair was, cascading down her slender back. Seeing that Syrinx had stopped by a river, he walked towards her, careful but determined. There was no way that she could swim that current, and if he did not frighten her, then soon she would be in his arms.

Syrinx raised her arms and Pan took this for a sign of surrender. Strange words were coming from her lips, as if she were intoning an invocation, but he rushed forwards, eager to hold her. The breeze blew her soft robe into his face and his arms closed - around empty air. All that was left was a clump of reeds through which the wind sighed forlornly.

Pan sat down beside the river, sad and perplexed, listening to the weird and mournful sounds of the reeds. Then he had an idea. His love might have gone from him, but he could make music. He carefully plucked selected reeds and bound them to make his pan-pipes. Then he walked slowly off, through the forest, playing the poignant strains that became his hallmark. The authors like this story because it tells of transformation - not only of Syrinx's physical shape, but also of purpose and energy. Pan, the Nature god, is telling us that if you can't succeed one way, then you will another, how to snatch success from the jaws of failure, how to be adaptable, how to accept, make do and get on with it. Pan is a lover, a loser, a pragmatist and a music maker.

A story from Plutarch tells how, some 2,000 years ago, a strange cry was heard in the Mediterranean, proclaiming 'Great Pan is dead'. However. Great Pan is very much alive in any man who recognises he is part of the Earth, who honors his sexuality as an expression of his sacred masculinity - and is prepared, when necessary, to make the best of a bad job!

Iron John

This story has been made famous by Robert Bly, who is listed in 'Further Reading'. We summarise it here.

Once upon a time there was a king, a queen and a prince, who was their son. They lived in a castle next to a dark and brooding forest. Men who went into this forest to hunt or chop wood were never seen again. Soon everyone avoided the place - but this was hard for the people, for they depended on the game and firewood to be had there.

One day a knight clattered across the castle drawbridge.

'Need anything heroic done, any dragons to kill?' he enquired, as knights do.

'Er well,' replied the king, 'it's funny you should ask, but we do have a little problem.' He went on to explain about the forest and the disappearances. Taking a dog with him, the knight rode fearlessly into the darkness of the wood, and quite soon the dog picked up a scent. The knight had to run fast to keep up with him, and was just in time to see his dog stop where the trail ended at a forest pool. An arm came up from the pool and pulled the dog under.

Seeing this, the knight returned to the castle and brought men with pails who emptied all the water out of the pool. There at the bottom was a Wild Man, the colour of rust, with hair matted down to his knees. They put him in chains and brought him back to the castle, where he was imprisoned in a cage, and the key to the cage was given to the queen. The Wild Man was called Iron John.

Things were much more comfortable for everyone now, except for Iron John. One day while the prince was playing in the courtyard, his golden ball went into the cage. He went up to

Iron John and asked for it back, but the Wild Man said he would only get it if the prince unlocked the cage door. Hesitatingly the young prince crept to his mother's bedchamber and stole the key from its hiding place beneath her pillow. Now the Wild Man was free, but the prince was afraid of his parents' anger. So Iron John lifted him up on his shoulder and they escaped to the wood.

Iron john looked after the boy well, but the boy failed to guard the special pool, as asked. Instead he kept dropping things into it and finding they turned to gold. So Iron John sent him out into the world, saying he would always be there for him in his hour of need.

This came after a while, for the castle where he had gone to make his fortune was under threat. The boy had been working as a kitchen hand and a gardener, concealing his hair - which had also turned gold - as best he could. But the princess, to whom he had brought wild flowers, knew of his splendid golden mane. Nonetheless the boy was not allowed to ride with the champions, who scorned him and left a three-legged horse for him in the stables, laughing that he could make his way to the battle as best he might.

The boy rode the poor nag to the forest and called for Iron John who appeared immediately with a magnificent horse and a troupe of fine knights. They rode to the battle where things were going ill for the king, who would have been defeated, except that the disguised Prince rode in to save the day. After the battle the boy went back to the forest, returned the horse and the knights, and wended his way home on the old three-legged mount.

Now the king was extremely anxious to find out who the mighty champion was who saved the day for him. So he organised a tournament where the princess was to toss a golden apple to the winner. The boy went to the forest and called Iron John who gave him red armour and a red horse. Duly victorious, the boy rode off with the spoils, unidentified, and the king was much put out. A second tournament was arranged, for which Iron John gave the prince white armour, and when again the same thing happened, a third tournament was put on.

'This time we shall see,' said the king. The disguised prince rode this time in black, and again he won. However, the king told his knights to ride after him, and they wounded him in the leg. He lost his helmet and his golden hair gleamed. When the princess heard this, she said she knew who the mysterious knight was - it was, in fact, their own gardener's boy.

A great feast was arranged to which the boy's parents were also invited, rejoicing to see their son again. And, as you can guess, the prince married the princess and they lived happily ever after. As everyone was sitting for the marriage feast the doors burst open and in walked a mighty king accompanied by a retinue of gorgeously dressed courtiers. You may have an idea who this was!

'I am Iron John,' announced the king. 'Through an enchantment I was turned into a Wild Man, and you have freed me. All I have now belongs to you.'

Commentary

This is a complex story and if you are interested we suggest that you read Iron John (see Further Reading) for the full examination. Here are a few pointers:

In a forest pool, in a deep, dark forest, lays an unredeemed figure that has become dangerous through neglect. He is leaching energy and life from the surrounding land. He is Iron John, the wild and instinctual side of a man's nature, so often repressed and denied and thus behaving destructively. Iron John, deep in the forest pool, leaves a man an impoverished, frustrated automaton. Every so often up comes the arm and the man is hauled down in a drinking bout/fight with boss or wife/car crash. This is what happens if our natural urges are unacknowledged.

The frequent appearance of gold suggests all the treasures here available. Gold comes upon the boy's head, indicating the acquisition of wisdom.

The key is under the pillow of the queen. Much in the way of the non-rational yet powerful is in the keeping of Feminine. This must be stolen in some way - you do not negotiate with instinctual, nor can a boy separate from his mother using a logical approach. This has to take place at a wordless level, hopefully with the help of other men. The 'key' is found with the Feminine, but the boy does not stay in his mother's bed! He has to break completely free from the unconscious domination of Mother/Feminine and find initiation with the Wild Man before he can return to unite with the Feminine as equal (having found his own wild side) by marrying the princess. Note he brings her wild flowers. The princess represents the 'anima' - the 'inner feminine' of the man, and while it is cold and clumsy to think of real women as signifying one's anima, yet the term has lots of meaning for inner balance.

Another way of looking at this may be that a man needs to be able to manage without the emotional support of women before he can enter into equal relationships. This is very important, for while the value of the Feminine is widely disparaged, yet there is a great, often unexpressed, tendency for men to depend on women for their emotional wellbeing.

The red, white and black colours of the armour suggests stages in the process of 'realisation and experience. Red means life, white may mean spirituality, Black Death. The boy is wounded before he finds completion. Until we are conscious of our mortality and our inner 'wounds' we cannot be complete. This may mean recognising lots of things about ourselves hitherto denied, for example we are often helpless, confused, afraid, petty, resentful, hateful, and that our childhood, however good it was on some levels, has left us with real inner wounds that may never completely heal. But that need not stop us, for strength comes from such realisations.

Iron John is king. The supreme power of a man lies in his deepest and most primitive recesses. The Wild Man can meet the Witch face to face and not back down, for each has access to the same energies. How may we describe this better? It is the kind of thing you know so well when you arrive at it, but it does not translate well into words. The Wild Man is prepared to face anything in himself and in the world. This does not mean being fearless; it means acknowledging fear and a lot more besides. He knows Where there's muck, there's brass' - or perhaps not brass, but the gold of the spirit.

Practice - the vision quest

In Native American tradition it is customary for young men to seek a spiritual experience at puberty, and this is usually done by going out into the wild and being alone with Nature. Preparation for this way may include fasting and sweat-lodge - it is usually arduous and scary.

It cannot be sufficiently stressed that it is foolish in the extreme to imitate the customs of people who are much wiser, hardier and more experienced than we are. Few of us can cope with the conditions that a native American might find commonplace, and if we try to, we are risking death. That isn't wise, or spiritual. Genuine seekers have respect for their own bodies and avoid causing anguish to others. Both the inexperienced and the experienced have been known to die on mountain, moor or in caves. However, we can seek special experiences, in modes that are compatible with our capabilities.

The requirements for your vision quest are simple. It needs to have an element of effort and challenge, it needs to involve you being alone with Nature or at least with carefully selected companions, and it needs preparation and the right attitude of openness and humility.

You may like to prepare for your 'quest' by eating as simply as possible for a few days beforehand. Steer clear of tea or coffee, and avoid alcohol or tobacco, and foods with many additives. Eat fruit, whole meal bread, nuts and such like. Some people like to abstain from meat, for all but the highest-quality, free-range organic meat is liable to be full of toxins. Also many people feel that eating animals is not desirable - it's up to you. You must not approach your vision quest physically weakened in any way, so eat heartily, but purely.

Before your quest take a bath with salt in it. Afterwards light a candle and formulate a prayer or request, such as 'I ask the gods of Nature to show me a vision, or bring me enlightenment'; 'May I see what I need to see, in the name of the Horned God and the Goddess' or anything that appeals.

Now go to the place you have chosen, for the time you have chosen, taking appropriate equipment, clothes and food. You may sleep out under the stars in a bivvy-bag, spend time in a Neolithic barrow or crop circle, make your own circle of stones and remain within it, or simply camp in a beautiful spot. You should not be disturbed for the length of time you have decided. Many people do such things anyway, but at this time you have a specific purpose. We repeat, no alcohol or tobacco, no books, radio or other distractions. Just you, the earth and sky and the minimum of needs.

If you need to be alone, it is best to take friends with you who will remain out of sight but within hailing distance. Needless to say, these must be people who understand utterly what you are doing, and aren't going to play practical jokes or disturb you. So much the better if you know a more experienced man who can guide you, and for this it might be worth contacting a shamming group or lodge to see if anyone can help - some resources will be found at the back of this book. However, you should always take the utmost care with any new group you contact, for while the vast majority are no doubt genuine, there will be the occasional person who wishes to exploit the unwary, for many reasons, and such may pose a real danger.

If you wish to sleep rough but are completely inexperienced then you should seek your vision with a group of like-minded friends. Or you may prefer not to stay out all night. Consult experts regarding what you will need - most scouts will able to give advice. Make sure that someone knows where you have gone and when you will be back.

Patrick Corbett, one of our contributors, regularly walks the Ridgeway, by night, with a friend. The Ridgeway is an ancient track starting at Ivinghoe Beacon near Tring in Hertfordshire, passing near Uffington White Horse in Oxfordshire and the Neolithic mound called Wayland's Smithy to end at Avebury. This is believed to be the oldest track in Europe, and is 96 miles in length. Walking this track is a type of vision quest, and seems a very suitable approach for men from Western culture. Those of you who do not live in England, or are too far from this track, can seek out similar paths, for these certainly exist in America, Australia and worldwide.

Time alone with Nature, walking, sitting meditating, listening to the sounds, breathing in the scents, sometimes literally brings forth visions. More usually it changes perceptions, perhaps quite subtly. You may notice a difference in your approach to life. Give yourself the space to see what happens. Afterwards you may like to record what has happened in a notebook, although it is unlikely you will forget it.

Chapter 4

Hunter, Warrior, Hero

*Odysseus, master of land ways and sea ways,
why leave the blazing sun, O man of woe;
to see the cold dead and the joyless region?
Stand clear, put up your sword;*

Homer, Odyssey

The 'warrior' is a frequently encountered model of masculinity. Books, plays, films and TV drama all regularly portray fighting in some form, and it is usually men who are involved. Despite the growing propaganda to the contrary, boys still feel they have to be tough, stand up for themselves, fight their own battles - and men cry much less frequently or readily than women. A deeply ingrained conditioning of men to be hard shows little sign of abating, and is encouraged by screen heroes who show no weakness, fear or ineffectuality.

Popular Heroes

Characters such as Rambo have a fascination for many young men. These may have a wound, or flaw, but this does not affect their ability to act as ruthless, efficient, killing machines. However, they probably have a soft spot for children and small animals - added to humour, this makes all the violence, explosions, blood and gore 'okay'. Other heroes for young males often include successful sports personalities - victors in their field. This is an awful lot for boys to attempt to live up to.

It is natural to feel satisfaction at the wholesale and gung-ho approach which destroys all opposition, for it appeals to the omnipotent infant in us. How nice to be able to smash all in our path! And isn't it satisfying that we know exactly who are the good guys and who are the bad guys? We don't have to question any of our own possible shortcomings, for it is easy to see who the villain is. Blow him up, crash his car, beat his head in or throw him off a tall building. It's cathartic to watch, and then we can all have tea. Generally, this is fairly harmless and amusing, but when accompanied by a complete lack of awareness or questioning it may be subtly destructive. Entertainment isn't reality, but when there is an absence of real-life role models and guidance, it may just contribute to problems. We can't be sure - but we all know that violence is a problem in our society.

Sports and show-biz personalities are 'real' but distance makes this reality very partial. Besides, someone who is brilliant at tennis or football, drums, keyboard or guitar, may be a most inadequate character at heart. With many fathers absent, either totally or partly, young males often seem hungry for someone to show them how to be a man - and when one is starving, almost any meal will do.

Achievement, Conquest, Campaign
Men are assessed quite often on the basis of the power they attain - or the money, which usually amounts to the same thing. External achievement is stressed - never mind about the inner man, what he may want, or who he may be. Many nations are still bent on conquest, and those that are at least making attempts to alter this, taking what purports to be a peacemaking and protective role, still speak of 'war on drugs', 'war on crime', as if there has to be a 'war' somewhere. In so doing, what is opposed is lent a subtle power, instead of a striving for wholeness, consciousness and understanding. Even in sections of society that are extremely peaceable, such things as 'sales campaigns' are regularly spoken of, and business revolves round competition and takeover. Indeed, the warrior approach is pervasive and deep rooted.

Historical Perspective
Opinions differ concerning the origins of human society, but it seems that man, by virtue of superior size and strength, took on the role of hunter, provider of meat and killer of dangerous animals, while woman gathered fruits and nuts, bore children and 'kept the home fires burning'. While it seems logical that those who could bear children should stay closer to the cave or hut, tending and feeding them, we may have extrapolated too far from this model. Many recent studies - for instance, of baboons - have shown that our perception of male primates as being eternally competitive, dominant and spoiling for a fight may appear so only through the lens of our preconceptions. Stone Age man may have undertaken the bulk of the hunting, but that does not mean he was aggressive. Hunting was a sacred activity - animals were, seemingly, much respected. And male animals rarely indulge in fights to the death.

Many avoid confrontations and there are often complex patterns of behaviour designed to avert such encounters. Grandmother monkeys may well be the 'authority' in jungle hierarchy. Our image of the male as eternal aggressor may need to be reviewed.

As civilisation progressed and agriculture was adopted, the function of the hunter receded. Many of us like to believe that early agrarian societies were largely peaceful, worshipping and living close to Nature, and that the need for fighting for the most part did not exist, or was at least marginal. However, as the Iron Age advanced, so the warrior ethic grew, along with a concept of powerful and warlike gods - and so also the image of sole Father-God, commanding, detached and often merciless.

A sense of possessing a unique identity, separate from the rest of creation, was no doubt a massive step forwards in human evolution, but along with this sense of 'self' came a sense of 'other'. That 'other' might have better lands and more cattle, so why not just go and take these riches, rather than working for them oneself? So men became fighters, again mostly because they were stronger and bigger than women, but also because they do not bear children, and so they had more liberty. However, many societies did have female warriors, and although women were often the 'prize' in conflicts, there can be no doubt that women also bear responsibility. Everyone has suffered, and perhaps it is time that we woke up to the fact that this attitude is extremely old fashioned.

In most parts of the world, combat isn't what it was. It is one thing to paint your face blue and ride into battle with your comrades about you, for issues that are fairly clear cut, such as protection of one's village and loved ones. It is quite another to be offered up as cannon fodder. The two World Wars have changed the face of battle forever, and now, in the nuclear age, the stakes are greater. Men, women, children and the planet itself are liable to be casualties of war. Ancient warfare was often a matter of style, strut and bluster (as in the animal kingdom) and sometimes issues were settled by single combat. Now everything has become much more deadly.

Effects on the Male Psyche

> We are the hollow men
> We are the stuffed men
> Leaning together
> Headpiece filled with straw

This quotation, from T. S. Eliot's *The Hollow Men*, has something to say about the male condition after aeons of being expected to fight. If you have to face the fact, continually, that you may sustain horrible injury, suffering and death; if you feel that the safety of all you love and value depends entirely on your courage and prowess; if you have to think of yourself as a fighting machine; if you feel that you can get what you need only by going out and taking it, perhaps from someone weaker: if you feel you must not show fear - then you cannot afford to feel. Indeed. you cannot afford to think very much either - and the army goes to lengths to make sure that soldiers do very little thinking for themselves. You become a 'hollow man', 'leaning together' with other warriors, but rarely achieving true closeness, and your head is 'filled with straw'. Straw is dry - it does not cry.

Sam Keen (see Further Reading) has much to say on this subject:

> For millennia men have been assigned the dirty work of killing and have therefore had their bodies and spirits forged into the shape of a weapon. It is all well and good to point out the folly of war and to lament the use of violence. But short of a utopian world from which greed, scarcity, madness, and ill-will have vanished, someone must be prepared to take up arms and do battle with evil. We miss the mark if we do not see that manhood has traditionally

required selfless generosity even to the point of sacrifice.

The above begs several questions, such as 'what is evil?' and 'is it really "utopian" to aim for a society without war, or is it common sense?' It also seems to fail to address the mistaken notion of 'honour' which has often meant a man has done what someone higher up the hierarchy has instructed, rather than thinking for himself and risking being called 'coward'. War could not be conducted without hierarchies.

However, there is no doubt that many, many men have been left with little choice, many have been heroic and countless have suffered. We ask a lot of men, with this history in mind, if we expect them suddenly to become spontaneous, warm, responsive, able to experience and express a full range of feelings, but also to remain reliable and protective - and these expectations persist.

Personal Perspectives

Writing this book has been an occasion for us to think deeply about our opinions on male aggression, territorialism and such like. Howard has this to say:

> I am far from being a violent man and I would always avoid conflict if I could. There is a far better approach to sorting things out and results are usually gained through talking and negotiation. I am also aware that I can't consider my wife my property. Teresa is an independent person and makes her own decisions. Besides, I think in terms of a Goddess and have a love and reverence for the Earth.
>
> Nonetheless, at a deeper level, there is a part of me that does feel that my wife is 'mine'. I feel that it would be up to me to defend her and the family, if it came to that point. Yes, I would be scared, but I would overcome this by being

as prepared as I could be, and as effectual. I know I could be ruthless - I would be as efficient as possible, and I could kill.

I regard women as equal and I wouldn't mind having a female boss. I don't expect necessarily to be the sole provider, and I wouldn't mind being provided for. Nevertheless, I feel that when the chips are down, it's up to me. Because of this I am conscious of a certain need to be 'tough'. I have to maintain a certain attitude to get by and to some extent this would be more difficult if I were to allow myself to get more emotional. Yes, I know I should perhaps show my feelings more, but somehow there isn't always the space.

Teresa says:

I believe strongly in a woman's ability to be fierce and assertive as well as gentle, caring and all the usual qualities and I wouldn't respect a man who didn't respect my independence. I am a 'feminist' - not an ideological one, but generally I think much harm has been done to all things feminine, and that has had terrible effects. However, I don't 'blame' men, or hate them as a species - far from it. In general I like men and find there is a touching vulnerability in them, despite outward appearances. I love and feel reassured by something I can only call 'focus' and 'strength' in a man, as well as gentleness.

However, I must say that I would not wish to be with a man I considered generally ineffectual. I define effectuality in a variety of ways - it's not about being always capable, and it certainly isn't about never showing emotions. But I like a man who identifies what has to be done, and then does it as best he can.

I really hate violence because this is a sad enough world, there is so much pain anyway and so many, many times we make it worse for ourselves. Often I feel haunted by the thought of all the people that are suffering in wars around the planet, but there isn't anything I can do. Nonetheless, I am aware that I could certainly be physically violent in some circumstances, notably if someone tried to harm my children. I fear I might not be very effectual in this. I do have to admit that I would expect Howard to protect us as best he could, and although I would help I somehow rely on him to be much more efficient at it. At a very primitive level I also have to admit that I wouldn't want to have children with a man who wasn't prepared to fight if the situation called for it.

We can see from these thoughts that the situation concerning male aggression is anything but simple. Dynamics exist at many levels - what we may think may not be the same as what we may feel, and what may be suitable in one situation may not be so in another. We don't say that how we feel is 'right' or even clear. What does seem clear is that men are in an ambivalent position, generally, expected in many cases to be strong, fearless, reliable, sensitive, caring and responsive all in one breath. These matters need a lot of reflection.

Homophobia

The male need/expectation of 'hanging tough' permeates many areas of human experience. The need to repress feelings and appear 'heroic' means that men have kept each other at a distance. After all, if you are affectionate you may seem weak, and others may exploit you. Thus men become overly dependent on women, because they are allowed and expected to get close to them, for sex. A man may not show his feelings, but can bask in the expressive feeling dimension of his partner. All the more need, then, to 'own' a woman, so one can be sure of getting what one needs, without showing neediness

- it can all be done in the name of conquest, again. This spoils the sexual encounter, so that it becomes one of invading and possessing the woman. Men see that this is not very pleasant for the one who is treated in this way, so they react by making sure they are not invaded by the needs of others, keeping other men at a distance, needing women more and more (but not always admitting it) and so the vicious circle is perpetuated.

This fear in men results often in homophobia, even literal 'queer-bashing'. Men fear being invaded and possessed by another man. They also fear that a need for closeness might be catching. Homosexuals are victimised as a way of fighting off one's inner vulnerability and neediness - even one's own latent homosexual feelings. There is an all-pervading fear of not 'being a man'. The armed forces discourage homosexuality because caring and closeness undermine the 'warrior' approach. However, men have a heart-rending inner need for closeness with each other, starting with their fathers. Also, fear and suspicion of homosexuals is quite without basis, for it seems that homosexuality is often linked with a delicate, subtle and highly creative approach. Homosexuals pose no threat whatever to 'straights' and homosexual love can be seen as Nature's own resourceful form of birth control on a crowded planet! It is a form of love that can show inner balance, for the homosexual does not seek a complement to his polarity in relationships. It may also be linked to shamanic gifts and heightened sensitivity. Quite simply, it is part of the spectrum of human tenderness.

The issues addressed by this book, including those in this chapter, seem equally relevant both to 'gays' and 'straights'. The main difference seems to be that gay men have often given the matter more thought. As homosexuals may be considered as standing apart from 'the system', they have the opportunity to review it from a different perspective. Coming out may take tremendous courage - possibly the sort of courage possessed by the true 'hero' which we shall be considering later.

Ironically, in a 'warrior' culture, combat offers the only permissible situation for men to cuddle each other. Bloodied comrades throw down their swords and fling their arms about each other, the goal-scorer is pawed and embraced - and what really happens in those long, rugby scrums? The sooner men feel able to let each other get close, to put their arms round each other, to feel contact with each other's bodies and feelings, the sooner some of the bad effects of the violent approach will recede. This can't be done in a hurry, for there is much embarrassment and taboo. However, fathers can start with their sons, having as much body contact as possible, sharing activities and embraces. Robert Bly observes in Iron John (see Further Reading) that a woman cannot teach a man how to feel - only another man can do that, and who better than the father?

Heroic Images

What are we left to play with in terms of the heroic, leaving images of violence aside, as many men are poignantly aware of wishing to explore? Graham Boston has this to say:

> ... As for heroes (and heroines) we certainly need more of those. During Neptune's passage of Capricorn * we have seen a few of them, apart perhaps from Madonna, exemplifying perhaps the victory of the feminine intelligence, willpower and independence in a male world, or Michael Jackson, whose trans-gendered, trans-racial, even trans-human persona offered fascination until the flawed human was found beneath the mask. Both reflect the triviality of the times and the vaulting of money, wealth and power for their own sake.

A truer hero would seem to be Nelson Mandela, who suffered in jail for over thirty years because of his convictions, yet remained positive that he would eventually see his vision come about, and dignified in adversity. On his release his tolerance, forgiveness and genuine desire for unity changed the destiny of a country more than any amount of rhetoric, exhortation or the inflation that most politicians resort to. Such a man is surely of relevance to both men and women as an example of fortitude, forgiveness and inner strength....

My heroes (I suppose that is what they are) are Christ, Buddha, Jung, William Blake, Samuel Palmer, (a visionary artist and follower of Blake), Gurdjieff, Steve Hillage (a visionary musician).

In our pampered Western society in which there seems little to fight for (except [against] apathy) it seems to be that there is less need for heroes, yet there is a greater need for people to set a good example, especially to the young.

*Author's note: Neptune, the planet of the visionary and the ideal, passing through pragmatic Capricorn might be interpreted as doing away with illusions, perhaps encouraging us to adopt materialistic hero-models or offering an opportunity to examine what is 'really' heroic - as we are trying to do here.

The classical hero who delights in conquest an is apparently never afraid and always powerful, is obviously irrelevant. What emerges is the importance of trying to be true to oneself, of honesty in self-expression, of trying to do what one is best capable of, whether one has a spiritual mission or an ability to build drystone walls. Heroism is an individualism that honours the individuality of others, and it comes through the most gruelling of processes and facing the most horrendous monsters - for it involves being honest with oneself and facing one's inner demons. Heroism is the triumph of consciousness that reaches into the inner pool to draw up gold. Perhaps the 'classical' hero has a meaning, after all.

The Hero's Descent

Many myths speak of the descent of a hero to the Underworld, there to face the most appaling perils and ordeals, to emerge triumphant and powerful into the light of day, laden with stolen treasure, This scenario has been taken all too literally, but Jung, the great exponent of myth as a metaphor for the inner workings of the mind, defined the true meaning of the heroic quest as a descent into the Unconscious and the bringing back of some of its contents into the light of consciousness, thereby making the personality more 'whole'. Anyone who has ever attempted a serious incursion into their own darkness, so to speak, is aware of how frightening and horrendous this may be. On a lighter level, facing our own repression, prejudices and shortcomings may be extremely painful, involving as it often does the realisation that we are exactly that which we have always hated, in some respect!

Let us look at one of the most poignant Greek myths of a man who braved the most fearsome realms for that which he loved, who lost his nerve at the last minute and remained unrequited.

Orpheus and Eurydice

Orpheus was a prince of Thrace. He had journeyed with the Argonauts on their voyage to steal the Golden Fleece, but he was no warrior. He was a poet and musician of rare talent. In fact so heartrending, so pure, so sweet was his music that animals would come from the forest to cluster about him as he

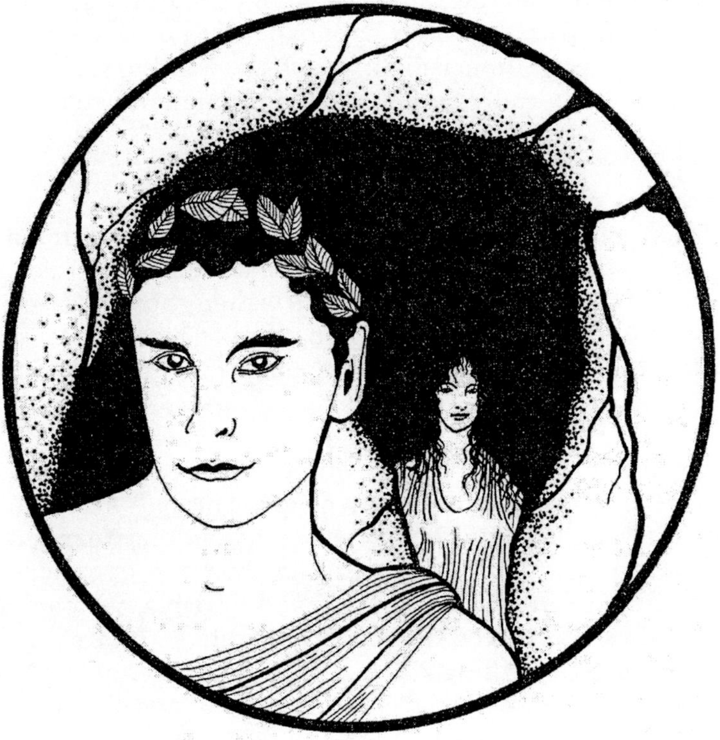

played, and even the trees would pull up their roots and the stones move of their own accord to be close to him.

Orpheus loved Eurydice, and she became his wife on his return from his voyages. She was all the world to him, and all his songs were sung for her alone. They spent several happy years together, until one day they received a visit from an old friend who took Eurydice for a walk and tried to seduce her. Eurydice ran from him in a panic and did not see a snake curled in her path. In her flight she stepped on the snake and was bitten. The deadly poison coursed through her veins and before Orpheus could get to her she was dead.

Thrace was plunged into mourning, its prince utterly bereft. Orpheus remained in his room, neither eating nor drinking, his lyre silent and his face as pale as that of his dead wife. At length he emerged, his cheeks still ashen, but dressed in traveller's garb. Orpheus was going on the most dangerous and taboo of journeys, for he was going to the Land of the Dead itself.

Long and hard was the journey, and Orpheus accomplished it through endurance and acts of magic. Through storm and mist, forest and mountain, by many twists and turns and byways at length he found himself in the Land of Shadows. The sights he saw were haunting and horrible, for endless tortures were inflicted on those whose lives had harmed others or offended the gods. At length he came, more dead than alive, before the thrones of Persephone and Pluto, king and queen of Hades.

The thrones were high, made of cold, black onyx. Persephone was veiled, and Pluto's face was in shadow. Around them clustered demons of the night with fearsome weapons - hordes upon hordes, stretching into the blackness. But Orpheus held to his purpose. Lifting his lyre on his ragged arm he began to play, and as he played he sang of his love for Eurydice, his longing and his quest. In poignant music he begged that she be returned to him.

At length Persephone removed her veils to show a face as pale as opal, glistening with tears. Even Pluto leant forward and Orpheus could see the depth of his great eyes. Persephone said to him solemnly and softly 'Musician, you have charmed our hearts. What you ask shall be yours, and Eurydice shall return, on one condition. You must leave this place and return to the surface without ever once looking behind you. Go now - your wife shall follow.'

The Queen resumed her veils and the shades fell again. Orpheus started for the upper world, invigorated and triumphant.

Behind him he could hear the soft footfalls of Eurydice, but he knew he must not look back. On and on he went, until it seemed he would never be out of this dreadful place. Surely the way in had not been so long? As he walked his doubts grew. What if the dark queen had lied? What if this was not Eurydice behind him, but some dreadful monster? Could he, should he, risk a peep?

Now the light was gaining. He was near the surface, and there the sunshine lay bright and reassuring. Now surely it would be all right to look? Just as he was about to take his first steps into the daylight, Orpheus turned around. Alas - if only he had waited. There was Eurydice, almost with his grasp. Their fingers touched as he reached out to her, but then with a scream that faded into the echoing distance she was gone - snatched back into the Underworld and lost to him forever.

Lost in despair and self-blame beyond description, Orpheus played his lyre beneath the trees, until at length he was not able even to do that. He remained as one turned to stone until, some legends say, a band of revellers tore him to pieces for his refusal to join them. Now at last Orpheus could journey again to the Underworld and be reunited with his love.

Commentary

It is an insult to this myth to examine it too thoroughly. It has many, many meanings. It speaks of heroism, failure, loss and new perspectives on death. It also tells of powers that have nothing to do with swords and physical force.

Don't give a sword to a man who can't dance

The story of Orpheus is one of a man who used all the talents he had to best advantage. He may not have danced much himself, but all people, all creatures danced to his beautiful music. He was a man in touch with life, who braved death.

The Celtic saying 'Don't give a sword to a man who can't dance' is very important. It means many things, but most especially it means don't give a sword or any weapon of destruction to a man who doesn't appreciate, at a deep level, the wonders of poetry and music, who cannot lose himself in the expression of delight, and, most of all, who cannot appreciate the dance of life in all its aspects. Such a man is the only man who should wield a weapon. If the value of life is understood ahead of the value of any conquest, few battles indeed would ensue.

Ways Forward

Here we make an attempt to discern some pointers. In respect of the 'campaign' aspect of companies and their sales, new approaches are vital which put human values ahead of commercial ones. This is rarely served by placing women in positions of power, for many women have had to become part of the hierarchical, upward-striving scheme of things and offer few new perspectives. Companies who do put human interests first, who attempt to make sure their employees are satisfied, who listen to them, who are not punitive about time off for illness, who support maternity and paternity leave and who regard it as essential that everyone is as happy as possible and valued - these companies find they are rewarded by high production and a good working environment, lower staff turnover and less illness. Pressure, tension, competition - these are all counterproductive. Perhaps seats on the board should only go to those who can dance - really dance.

In respect of the 'heroic', men should feel able to give themselves permission not to be heroic in any traditional way. Men should be able to feel they can be scared, confused, unable, and still be 'okay'. The pacifist may be more heroic than the fighter, the patient in analysis braver than the racing driver.

If there is a need for conquest and striving in some form in the male psyche - which we think may well be the case - then it should perhaps be used as a 'Rainbow Warrior' for the cause of the Earth, fighting peacefully - if that is not a contradiction in terms - striving positively, not hurting people, property or institutions but using efforts always to achieve more openness, honesty and balance.

Masculine incisiveness can be used to cut through the 'Gordian Knot' of confusions and evasions, not in a spirit of righteousness, but with the mind of the earnest seeker. Above all, one of the most heroic quests must be as defined by Jung and exhorted in the mystery cult of Eleusis in ancient Greece: 'Know Thyself'.

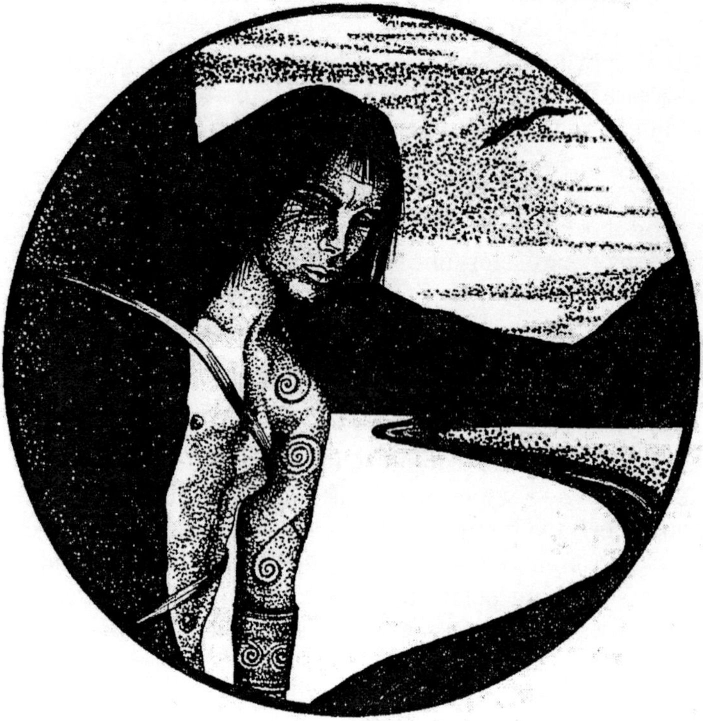

Bearing in mind these considerations, let us turn to a tale of prowess and bravery, adapted and abridged from Irish lore.

Cuchulain's Last Battle

Cuchulain was the mightiest hero Ireland had ever known. Son of the Sun god, Lugh Longhand master of craftsmanship, he could roll before him a burning wheel, so that marshland dried up beneath his feet. When his battle-fever was upon him, blood spurted from his forehead and sparks flew around his great head. To cool him down, maidens would greet him bare breasted, to remind him of the gentler values, and he would be submerged in three baths of cold water. The first he burst, so great was his heat, the second boiled away and with the third the hero finally returned to normal. This was an offspring of the Sun god, indeed.

Cuchulain loved Emer, who was not only the most beautiful woman in Ireland. but also the cleverest. She was her husband's equal for wit and courage and often made decisions on his behalf. To win her, Cuchulain trained in the arts of war with the warrior goddess, Scathach, on the Isle of Shadows. Their life together was happy, but portents had always foretold that Cuchulain's life would be short.

Now, because of an enchantment laid upon them for their disrespect to the goddess Macha in childbirth, a great weakness came yearly upon the men of Ulster. For five days and four nights they remained unable to move, vulnerable to attack. And it was upon one such occasion that their foes approached them. Cuchulain, being the son of no Earthly father, was exempt from the weakness, but he was susceptible to enchantment of his own. A spell laid on him by his enemies caused him to hear the sounds of battle, and he determined to ride out to the attack.

Emer clutched him and begged him with tears and caresses not to go. She explained that he was under a spell and that he had to wait for only a day and the men of Ulster would be up again, to ride at his side. Meanwhile the enemy hosts were too far away to pose a threat. But Cuchulain could hear the clash of steel and the cries of men, and he would not listen. His faithful charioteer, Laeg, yoked his warhorses, the grey of Macha and the black Sanglain, but they snorted and strained at the bit, and their great eyes were full of fear and sorrow.

Cuchulain went to his mother to ask for blessings for the coming battle, and she gave him wine, but when he drank the cup was full of blood. A second and a third cup turned also to blood. Cuchulain rode out to battle, and there a pale woman sat, keening by the riverside, washing Cuchulain's own bloodstained clothes. 'Alas,' said he to his charioteer, 'I fear we may not return with brave tales from this day, but may instead go to the Land of Shadows. But Laeg, I cannot turn back now. If I do, all the heart will go out of Ulster.'

With his warhorses at full gallop, Cuchulain came down upon the foe like a great wind. His battle fever possessed him and the blood spurted from his temple, falling around and behind him like red rain. Around his head fire played as if the Sun had come to Earth. Into the host he swept like a scythe, and enemies fell in their hundreds. But today the odds were too great even for the hero. Laeg and the horses were vanquished and Cuchulain was battered and torn. Knowing his last hour had come, the hero tied himself to a standing stone, facing west and the setting Sun. He would not die lying down, but would stand and meet his fate. Around him his sword swept in a crimson crescent, but the magical fountain had dried in his temple and his mouth was full of his own thick, human blood. His body was wracked with his wounds. A red mist swam before his eyes and he thought he could see the pale faces of the Sidhe beyond his attackers, with the form of Lugh towering above, his spear dazzling as the Sun.

Lugaid cut off his head, for the Irish valued heads as trophies being the seat of wisdom and eloquence. But the triumph of the victors was short lived. for now at last the men of Ulster rose from their beds and thundered to avenge their hero.

Emer received the news of her husband's death in silence. Quietly she rose and came to the place where his body still slumped and her face was the colour of the stone that supported him. She picked up the head of Cuchulain where it lay, returned by the Ulstermen. Carefully she washed it, wrapped it and held it to her breast, crooning over it as if it were a baby. Then she said 'Dig a wide grave, men of Ulster, for I will not live after my love.'

Cuchulain was buried in the earth. Emer lay beside him, pressed herself to his body and breathed her last breath into his cold lips. The great hero had gone, but down through many a long year his name was sounded in song and poetry, a battle-cry of freedom, loyalty and courage. The people of Ireland say Cuchulain still rides out from the faery mounds, the hosts of the Sidhe all around him in the Samhain twilight. And beside him rides Emer, her long, red hair streaming behind her in the mist, like a burning brand.

Practice

You may like to ask yourself how you define a hero, and what you think of the 'warrior culture'. Have you been forced into pseudo-heroic, 'tough' roles that are not an expression of you? Who are your heroes, and why? And would you define or seek the heroic in yourself?

Concerning violence, do you think there are ways to overcome the problem of violence in the world? What might they be? How do you/might you cope with violence? How would you like to cope with it? Is there an ideal to which we might progress?

Chapter 5

Reclaiming Roots and valuing the feminine

> ... And she sang out the hymn of his returning. From a distant star she saw him and when at last he arrived their meeting was complete, for through the parting had they become each a piece o f the other. And from the point of greatest darkness to the time o f greatest light did they unfold the edges of their story and plant seeds into the ground
>
> Carolyn Hillyer, *'The Fish and The Moon'* from the album Heron Valley, Seventh Wave Music, 1993

Many men are most explicit about their need to find the 'feminine' within themselves, and to honour it in the women they know and in the world at large. As we have seen, men have a side that could be called 'feminine' - Jung's 'anima'. In the same way women have an inner masculine, the 'animus'. Because of the largely dependent position of women historically, they have had to learn a lot about men, and so have learnt much about themselves. Men seeking equal knowledge of human nature might well be advised to do likewise.

Great numbers of men are deeply ashamed at the historical treatment of women, and some feel very guilty and almost personally responsible for every rape, witch burning and wife sale that has ever happened. It has been said that at present women are 'about' rage and men are 'about' grief. Much of this grief is loss of the more sensitive, wild, emotional and responsive aspects of maleness, that have been repressed for thousands of years, and also loss of true bonding with the Feminine, within and without. Janet and Stewart Farrar (see Further Reading) write:

> 'Even the God has suffered, for without his complement he is emasculated, his image distorted and impoverished ... Both the readmission of the Goddess and the reassessment of the God are essential to health on all levels ...'.

Fred Rosado, Resident Guardian of the Chalice Well in Glastonbury, recently said to Teresa and her friend Jane (our illustrator) 'For all that we have done, we can only say "We're sorry"'. This was a touching statement, delivered with great sincerity, and it seems Fred was speaking for many others. Of course, individual men are not to blame for what has happened, but we all have a responsibility to see that change comes about - and that change begins on the inside of each of us.

Sadism In The Male Psyche

Men have been accused of much cruelty. Is this fair? Really there can be no reason to believe that men are more sadistic than women, but history has given them more opportunity and more pressure.

Nicholas Mann, in His Story (see Further Reading), bravely describes certain feelings that no doubt are shared by many men:

> ... when I was reading about a rape o f some women by soldiers in the Vietnam War ... I realised that a part of me was getting a thrill from it. I was actually enjoying it. At the same time some other part of me knew that I should have been denouncing the rapes and striving to stop them. And some other part o f me was appaled and disgusted that I could be deriving any kind of fascination and pleasure from reading about it at all.

To many men, women represent that which fascinates, and is also frightening. The mystery of the intuitional, the primal, the wordless, the secret litanies, the dark pleasures of female body-knowledge beckon and tantalise - and what does any gung-ho hero do but follow, sword in hand, to claim and subdue? Of course, the fact that such matters cannot be conquered in this way only makes the pursuit more violent, in some personalities. And then there is the fear element - will I be swallowed in the black maw of the Great Mother, will I lose my uniqueness, my ability to think in a linear, objective way, if I get too close? Most men would not articulate their unease in this way, but many are also at least dimly aware that they are scared that if they get too close to a woman they will lose something. Fear breeds aggression, and both sexes have suffered. No man driven to violence assuages his inner thirst. Because men have been the 'master sex' their capacity for cruelty has often been highlighted, and they have had opportunities to indulge it. Man as a sex is not to blame, but perhaps systems such as patriarchy are. Cruelty is sanctified in many myths. Homer's *Odyssey* tells of the massacre of the suitors who had been besieging Penelope, wife to Odysseus, while he was away. This was the fate of Melanthius:

The two men pounced upon him, dragged him in by the hair and threw the unhappy wretch on the floor, where they tied his hands and feet together with biting knots, relentlessly forcing the limbs till they met behind him, as their royal master had ordained. Finally they made a rope fast round his body and hauled him aloft up a pillar till he nearly touched the roof .... Next Melanthius was dragged out across the court and through the gate. There with a sharp knife they sliced his nose and ears off; they ripped away his privy parts as raw meat for the dogs, and in their fury they lopped off his hands and feet.

This makes sickening reading - and note that such atrocity was decreed by the great hero, Odysseus, who by all accounts had been no better than he should have been while on his travels! It is an example of how brutality has been accepted as part of the warrior culture, and certainly the classical Greeks were patriarchal and warlike in nature. What are we to make of this?

It isn't our place here to examine the psychology of sadism, but we have observed that cruelty often stems from fear, and one of the mainsprings of fear is perception of our mortality, and our feeling of alienation from the natural world. To an alienated consciousness 'doing it to them before they do it to us' seems a good strategy. To a holistic consciousness, 'doing it to them' is tantamount to having it done to oneself -'holy' perception sees that we are all brothers and sisters, and that includes humans, animals, trees, flowers, rocks and crystals too. As the native North Americans say Mitakuye oyasin - 'All my relations'. What affects one affects all - we all suffer in our brother's pain.

Historical Comments

Many writers and historians believe that in the Stone Age humankind lived in a state of mystical unity with the natural world and the cosmos. As this was left behind in the development of individual consciousness, so the 'oneness' - that eternal, comforting feeling of being 'okay' contained in a meaningful totality where whatever came to pass made sense - was lost, hence alienation, separation, loneliness of the spirit, fear - probably this is the meaning of 'fall from grace', and from this may have stemmed scapegoating, human sacrifice and need for conquest.

Having lost a sense of all-pervading deity, meaning has left the world, which now seems threatening, inhabited by unpredictable and dangerous forces that need to be propitiated. Conquest of the territory and possessions of others may distract us from our vulnerability and may make us feel powerful for a while. Besides, when we have lost a sense of holism, polarisation results. The mystic sees subject and object as a unity, but when this is no longer available we may feel intense desire for union with something or someone, to make us feel complete. In the end nothing ever does make us feel 'complete' but the effort to gain it may give rise to much strife.

This sense of alienation seems to some extent a male issue, for women have long been seen as possessing 'intuition' and similar qualities - although it is most certainly not solely a male problem. Regaining a sense of holism is part of the quest to reunite with the Feminine, to rediscover the ancient Great Mother, to get back to soil, seed and root, and to grow anew from a solid base.

Masculine and Feminine

We are aware that even in using these terms we are on shaky ground! Many feminists insist that women do not have to think in terms of finding their inner masculine to become assertive and strong. This view is supported by myth and history, when we think of the Amazons, Queen Boadicea of the ancient Britons, the Celtic warrior goddess Scathach who trained heroes, the Egyptian lion headed Sekhmet, and others.

Similarly, men may assert that they do not have to find their inner feminine in order to develop sensitivity, responsiveness, intuition, gentleness and other characteristics traditionally represented by women. Our standpoint is that assertiveness, purposeful and direct action and certain types of strength come more easily to men, while to women sympathy, caring and receptivity flow naturally. The Farrars write:

> 'the masculine principle'... represents the linear-logical, analysing, fertilising aspect, with its emphasis on Ego-consciousness, and individuality, while the feminine principle represents the cyclical intuitive, synthesising, formative, nourishing aspect with its emphasis on the riches of the Unconscious. In human terms, these two principles can be said to correspond to the left-brain and right-brain functions respectively.

Nicholas Mann (see Further Reading) defines the matter visually:

> If a simple spatial differentiation were to be made between the archetypal feminine and the archetypal masculine it would be one where the former was concerned with horizontal space, with the centre to the circumference, and the latter with vertical space, the axis connecting the centre with the above and below. Men are concerned with vertical paradigms, ascent structures and linear movements. Women are concerned with paradigms which emphasise lateral movement, localised power and relationships.

So it seems that either approach remains two-dimensional without the other. One of our contributors, who is a social worker, has this to say:

> As one of the men in a predominantly female ... work setting I feel that I offer a possibly more practical and detached way of approaching many of the complex issues we, as a social-work team, are obliged to deal with. I sometimes feel that my female colleagues disempower clients by being overprotective and taking rather too much responsibility for clients, whereas I tend to do for my clients what they cannot, for whatever reason, do for themselves, or point them in the right direction.

Here we have a contrast in the male and female approach, where both are able to be effectual in a caring context.

We would also say that men seem to have a 'doing' consciousness, while women may be more about 'being'. Whether this is innate or as a result of conditioning, we cannot say, but we have a sneaking suspicion that there are basic differences between the sexes that are innate, and that are generally described in the ways given above. Just as there are physical differences, so it seems reasonable that there should be temperamental differences. This is our standpoint, but it isn't a rigid bastion that we seek to defend at all costs - it's our way of talking about things at the moment. So it seems understandable to explore men developing a feminine side and women developing a masculine one. All this means is that we seek inner balance. In the end, masculinity and femininity may be impossible to describe, for the reality seems to flow between and around all adjectives, like water between the fingers - it is an undefinable 'something' but it is there. Perhaps it is essentially a mystery - and mysteries send us on quests.

The Value of the Feminine For Men

'Femininity' represents basis, containment and source. It enshrines the virtues of gentleness, empathy, compassion and acceptance. In *The Crone Oracles* (Weiser, 1994) Ransom and Bernstein write:

> ... When people take a male body they are challenged on a personal basis to learn what it takes to be an active co-creator and participant in the outer world. Men must be able to relate and honour the feminine side of themselves and the women in their lives. They must be able to surrender and bond to the feminine so they can be regenerated, renewed and healed. Then they must take this knowledge and recreate or restructure the world with it ...

The difference between the feminine approach and the masculine approach to finding God, is that on the feminine path one would encourage another human being to find a direct experience of the Divine, however that may develop. On the masculine path, one must adhere to certain tenets or dogma.

Christ knew that the coming years would require the masculine form of tribal warfare and masculine-centred cultures to exhaust civilization's negative karma. He chose twelve male apostles because these men needed to be initiated into the feminine ... the Christ consciousness - the consciousness of the feminine polarity of the open heart ... If you carefully review Christ's relationships with the women you'll find he treated Mary Magdalen as an equal. Later in the book the authors go on to state: We would not have accomplished the industrial and technological revolution had we not subscribed to the male process of energy ... So it is not to be scoffed at, vilified or condemned.'

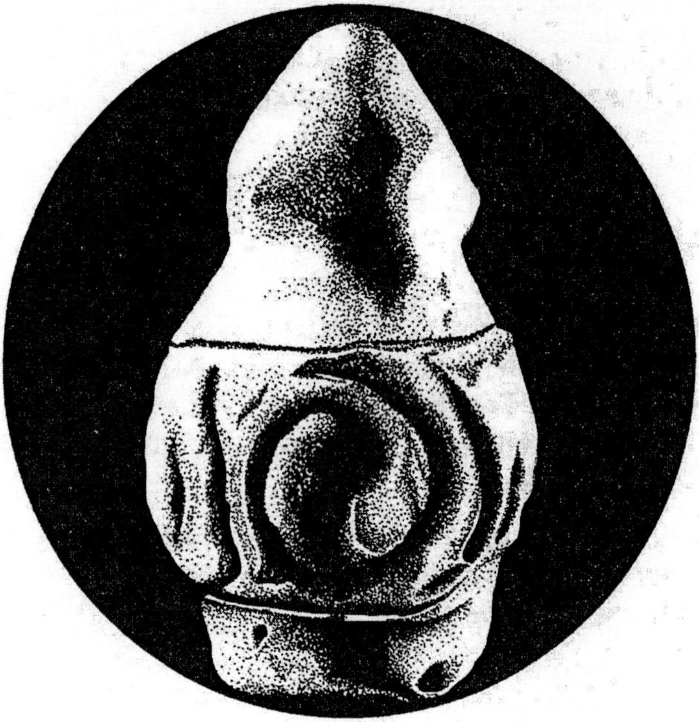

We feel this is an important quote for it shows a clear value for masculine talents, while encouraging us to re-find and reconnect to the Feminine. This seems to be in line with the feelings and wishes of many contemporary men. It is also behind many myths, For instance, the Grail Quest of Arthurian legend is a quest for the Feminine. The Grail is a symbol for the womb, the containment and acceptance of the Feminine, and the nourishment. Arthur's knights have become overbalanced on the masculine polarity and must find redress. In his book *He*, Robert Johnson mentions the 'Grail hunger' of young men. This is mostly unconscious, and shows itself often by provocative acts, such as fast driving or fighting. At some level, young men have a 'wound' to their sensuous, instinctual natures that may be healed only after a long quest to find their lost 'feminine'.

Arthurian stories also feature the Sword in the Stone. Again, the stone is a feminine symbol, being of the land. The King acquires his power to rule from the land - the union of monarch with land was the 'Sacred Marriage' of former eras. The function of the King is to honour and guard the land, and this is a sacred trust, conferred by the land - or rather the Goddess - herself. At length the sword is cast into another 'feminine' medium, into the waters. However, the sword - symbol of puissance and assertion - is available intact to all men who will seek within. The power within land and waters is something that, as a species, we need to rediscover, appreciate and cherish.

Patrick Corbett, occupational therapist in mental health, feels that establishing a connection to the Feminine is vital to men, and lack of this is a cause of ill-health. He says:

'In my work I see a lot of young males who can't cope with gender and are needing a connection with the feminine. Although I am aware that many psychologists may not agree with me, I feel that many go into serious mental disturbance as a result.'

Going down 'into the earth' to search for the rooted side of oneself and one's mother is important. This is not so much a question of relationship to the personal mother - although a good rapport here (as distinct from overdependence) is an advantage. It is a matter of Mother as a quality within and as an earthing and containing force. Perhaps the best way to express this is 'Goddess'.

The Goddess

As women have revitalised their perception of the Goddess, in Her single form and Her myriad manifestations, so also many men are strongly drawn to the Feminine, in deity. One of our contributors, who has a partly Christian background, writes of Mary - goddess in all but name - as follows:

> [Mary] ... was even more approachable [than her Son] and I sensed that in a way I could not verbalise that she was immensely strong, powerful and nurturing; and I felt that she was the creatrix in a way her son could never be ... In contemporary life I feel that what I have to offer is a gentleness and tenderness which enhances rather than 'debases' my masculinity.

Some men feel deeply saddened at their exclusion from groups of women worshipping the Goddess, and while women can hardly be blamed for this, many feeling emotionally unsafe in mixed company, there seems little doubt that the 'Goddess-shaped yearning' defined by Geoffrey Ashe is present in men, as well as women. It is outside the scope of this book to consider goddesses, but there are many books available on the subject, and one, The Goddess - a beginner's guide, has been published by Hodder Mobius. If men can forgive the feminist themes of many such books, they may find much to inspire them. They may uncover ideas to explore with other men, or in their own hearts, as our correspondent above has found in Mother Mary.

The Ancient Great Mother

Many writers and historians take the view that in the Stone Age worship of a Great Mother was almost universal, and although She may have been known by many names, many images and faces, yet She was essentially the same, in primeval forest, plain, cave or mountain peak. It certainly seems reasonable that this should have been so, for as life was seen to emerge from the females of all species, so all of the manifest world flowed from the womb of the Mother, returning there at death or dissolution, to be born anew.

As time progressed, the male role became more obvious in procreation. Women were still the keepers of the sacred, embodying it physically in their own selves, enacting it in daily life, in the sowing of seeds, the weaving of cloth, the making of pottery. Culture centred upon the women and children, while the men hunted and no doubt occupied themselves with other creative pursuits, more on the periphery. It is unlikely that the nuclear family had been thought of, but tribal society possessed its own binding factors of loyalty and communal support. Rituals to heal the rupture of the sacred continuum of life, which was felt to take place in the hunt, served to maintain humankind's sense of its rightful place in the cosmos. It is probable that this status quo prevailed for many, many thousands of years, until, as we mentioned above, a greater consciousness of separate self ushered in eras of conquest, war and domination. This sounds dire, and indeed there is no doubt that our race has been suffering under the Iron Age model of strife for far too long. However, in the development of unique consciousness, this was probably an unavoidable phase. Now, for humankind to survive, we need to progress beyond this model, and part of this process is the rediscovery and reanimation of our ideas of the Great Mother - certainly not to return to ancient ways, but to learn from what was valuable then, so a synthesis can take place and new visions be born.

What may this mean for men? There seems little doubt that some men find the image of an all-enveloping Great Mother rather more difficult to accept than women, who are able more readily to reach below and beyond the confines of 'rational' thought to the fertile, accepting strata, where distinctions merge and all begins and ends. However, we feel that men do need to find some way of relating to the Great Mother concept in order to plant the tree of their masculinity where it will flower to best advantage. Modern men are in a different position from modern women - women may forge ahead with the discovery and growth of images of the Feminine, while men have to disassemble the rigid, trapping constructs of patriarchy before they may find more complete and liberal expression. In this they can learn from women, and also from their own conception of, and relationship to, whatever Goddess-form appeals. In the end they can develop something that can enhance and strengthen their masculinity and their completeness as human beings.

The Feminine as First

There seems to be something more 'basic' about femininity. The foetus, in the womb, is female before it is male, and maleness arises as an 'extra' - male organs develop as the female ones atrophy and become vestigial - they are still there in a man, in some sense (as, of course, male organs are present vestigially in females, but that is another story). In the same way that women may need to access 'masculine' qualities to reach forwards to their full potential, so men may need to reach backwards, to contact the deep, primary Feminine. In *The Wise Wound* (Harper Collins, 1986) Shuttle and Redgrove describe man as 'the waterfly of existence'. In order to delve below the surface, to find firm foundation, men need to develop a sense of the depths of the Feminine.

It may strike men as unfair that the Feminine has to be considered 'first'- but 'first' does not mean 'superior', except perhaps in linear-logical idiom! It refers to order of remembering and reassembling. We suggest that little can be accomplished in the way of a more meaningful image of masculinity if an attempt is not made to return to and retrieve the image of the Feminine. Men need perhaps to appease this aspect before there can be firm ground on which to build.

It must also be said, however, that men do need to get away from dependence on women in order to find a true form of contact. As we saw in the tale of Iron John, the key is taken from under the pillow of the Queen mother. She holds the key, temporarily, but she does not keep it. The young prince uses it as a way out into a world that tests and rewards him. In not understanding closeness and sensitivity men may become overly dependent on women, yet still unsatisfied. A way needs to be found to understand, find the key and then, at length, find one's way back, as the prince does when he marries the princess. Now contact can be conscious and mutually satisfying. Independence and real love can be found by acknowledging such feelings as vulnerability and learning to cope with them oneself before uniting with another.

The Great Mother as Androgyne

A multitude of images of the Great Mother have come down to us, represented by symbols, shapes and animals. One of the favoured, and probably earliest, of these images is that of the bird. The bird mediates between earth and sky, and a waterbird also dives beneath the waves. A bird appearing from out of the blue is a metaphor for the mysteries of manifestation, and the emergence of a baby bird from an egg is a creation motif.

The inspiring point about symbols is that they cannot be confined - they speak many languages, sing many songs. Images of the Great Mother may depict a bird with a long neck. Similarly, the serpent with its spirals is another symbol of passage into and out of the visible world. Both the serpent and the long-necked bird can be seen as phallic symbols.

It has been suggested that the early Great Mother was androgynous - as source of All, She had no specific gender. In *The Myth of the Goddess* (Arkana, 1993) Cashford and Baring write:

> The mystery of the female body is the mystery of birth, which is also the mystery o f the unmanifest becoming manifest in the whole of nature. This far transcends the female body and woman as carrier of this image, for the body o f the female o f any species leads through the mystery of birth to the mystery of life itself.

In 'the mystery, of life itself' men too partake, as much as women, not just in their procreative power but in their essence as sentient, creative beings. Our forebears, with their rich, symbolic imagination could surely not have missed the phallic nature of the sacred shapes they created, even if they were unaware - which we doubt to some extent - of the male role in procreation. (Ancient people, who observed the heavens with a sophistication which is only slowly becoming apparent to us, quite possibly had some idea that the pleasurable and unifying activity of lovemaking had something to do with conception and birth!)

Men wishing to reconnect with their most primal source might like to contemplate some of this ancient imagery, which is concerned with mysteries too deep for words. This is addressed in our Practice section.

The Tower

This harrowing Romanian myth illustrates how ideologies, blind beliefs and patriarchal determination to strive and achieve have been friend to neither men nor to women:

Once upon a time, in Transylvania, there was a great bishop who decreed that a magnificent church should be built upon an ancient sacred site he had found. He assembled all the finest craftsmen to build this monument to his God. Diligently and with devotion they began work upon the edifice - but a strange thing happened. Each day they laboured nonstop, and each night all they had done was demolished. Dawn would find the walls in ruins, and they would have to start again. This went on for three years, until the bishop asked the chief mason, Kelemen, what was happening. Kelemen explained the mystifying events, whereupon the bishop told him he would spend the following night in prayer, and would let them know God's message in the morning.

Well, the old bishop spent most of the night on his knees, and no answer came. As morning approached he fell asleep, and a dream came to him in which a dark figure explained what must be done.

'The walls are falling because of an old curse from pagan times. The only way the curse can be broken is by walling up a young woman alive, in the masonry - then the building can be constructed.'

Being a man of literal belief, the bishop did not question the vision. The next morning he instructed the masons that they must bury one of their wives alive in the stone. Now there were ten masons altogether and they all had young, pretty wives, and many had babies. Kelemen, the leader, told them that the first woman that came with food for them the next day must be sacrificed, and he made them all swear not to tell their wives. But the young men were in love, and besides this seemed far too dreadful to contemplate. All of them, except Kelemen, whispered to their beloved not to come the following day.

Kelemen was a man of duty. He loved Piros, his wife, dearly, but he would not disobey directly. Instead he gave her many complicated instructions that were sure to delay her coming to him - surely, surely, his darling wife would not be the one to be buried alive in the cathedral.

But Kelemen had reckoned without his wife's love and determination. Despite all obstacles she made her way to him, with her new babe, only two weeks old, held to her breast. She was late, so late. The Sun was high in the sky and it was almost noon, but still she could not let Kelemen go without breakfast. Tired but happy, Piros stumbled into the dusty yard and gave her husband his food package. She did not see the grim and stricken look on his face, as she bent to suckle her crying baby. But then one of the masons wrenched the baby from her breast and placed her on the wall, tying her feet to a stump of broken masonry. Piros thought this must be a joke, and cried to Kelemen to stop them.

'What are they doing,' she wept, in growing panic, as the stones rose around her. Her full breasts flowed in response to her baby's cries. Soon the stones began to hurt her, she could not breathe properly, the light of the Sun was hidden as the masonry grew around her. 'Kelemen, Kelemen, how can you let them do this to me? What about our baby? Kelemen, let me out, let me out.' Soon all her cries were muffled, and she did not hear her husband when he answered, through his sobs: 'The fairies will nurse our babe, the wind will rock him and the rain will bathe him.' Kelemen held his crying child stiffly, while the muffled shrieks went on and on and on.

The walls rang intermittently with the mother's desperate screams, but after three days, all was silent. Even the wind did not blow now over the building site, or the birds fly above it, but the walls rose apace and soon the great church stood fine and solid, as the bishop had planned. Now the bishop should have been grateful, but he heard the men whispering about what they had done to Piros and he realised that the terrible secret would never be safe. So, while all ten men were putting finishing touches to the roof, he took away the ladders and the scaffolding so the men were stranded high in the clouds.

Now the men screamed and shouted but the bishop left them to their fate. But these were resourceful craftsmen. Led by Kelemen they fashioned wings from pieces of wood that were left on the roof and one by one they flew into the air. However, a strange thing happened, for although their wings worked perfectly, none of them reached the ground, for they all turned to stone on the way down. Kelemen, seeing what had happened to his companions, sorrowed and wondered. He tried to make himself better wings, but he caught his foot and crashed down, hitting his head on a rock by the church foundations, where his Piros was buried. He died instantly. Or perhaps Kelemen, who was after all only a sad, misguided man who had let hierarchy and mistaken sense of duty come between him and his heart, flung himself from the rooftop in despair, so that he might join his wife.

A little brook started up from the spot where he fell - some say this was the tears of Piros. We believe that the tears were from both Piros and Kelemen, now reunited in an existence free of misunderstanding and blind adherence to cruel laws. As for the old bishop, we hear no more of him, but we may be sure the dark figure of his dreams will be waiting for him each time he closes his eyes.

Commentary

Few comments need to be made about this story, which shows terrible damage done to women, men and the sacred. The metaphors of being walled up alive, stranded high above the earth and turning to stone are quite obvious. Let us pretend that the cold, grey walls can be pulled down, that Piros may rise anew from them, that Kelemen may come back to life and the masons that were turned to stone can again become human. Now the Sun can shine, birds can fly and the breeze play over the sacred grove - and let us pretend that all the masons and all their wives can dance and celebrate there, by the light of the Moon, in the heat of the Sun. A simple, idyllic image, perhaps, but a hopeful one for our future.

Practice

There are several themes to ponder from this chapter. How do you feel about a Goddess? Are you able to imagine Her? What feminine images might inspire you, and how might they help you? How might finding your own feminine side help you as a man and a person? Do you feel you need to reconnect with your feminine side and improve your relationships with women - and other men? Where, in your working, studying or other day-to-day environment, could better appreciation and incorporation of feminine principles help? And if you are a man who already feels a strong connection to the Feminine, how does this affect your relationships with other men? Are you able to help them? Or do they misunderstand? How might this be improved?

Here is a visualisation exercise that you might like to try, to feel more connected to your source. To embark on this you will need to be sure that you won't be disturbed for about half an hour. You will need to be warm and comfortable and you will need to relax, in whatever position suits you. You may prefer a darkened room, or candlelight, and some people like to burn incense. It will help if you can record the exercise on to a tape, with plenty of pauses. When you are completely relaxed you can begin:

You stand in a forest grove. Around you the trees are thick and the greenery luxuriant. This looks like a semi-tropical place, or a primeval forest such as covered the lands many thousands of years ago. Take your time and look about you, noticing all the plants, and any other life there may be.

Short pause.

Now you notice a small cave ahead of you. It is dark, and hardly big enough to enter, but you feel drawn to it. As you approach, a smell of ancient stone, deep, earthy mysteries, seems to enter you, and you feel even more strongly attracted to the cave, although you also feel a small thrill of fear. Slowly, in your own time, approach the cave. Lower your head and shoulders and begin to go in. It is very, very dark. The sides of the cave are muddy. Your body slithers in fairly easily, but there is little room to move and no room to turn.

Short pause.

'Twisting and sliding, you enter deeper and deeper into the earth. It is pitch dark. You are conscious of strange and primitive scents. You know you cannot turn around- or pull-yourself backwards and upwards, and you may feel scared, but you do not panic. Something tells you you are safe and held by a power that you cannot describe or understand, but this is a power of Love. Continue to slither deeper, taking note of your feelings and sensations.

Short pause

Now you are conscious that the tunnel is widening. Slowly, slowly the space in which you are moving grows, and a faint light is appearing ahead. You push on, until you can stand.

Now you walk, head bent at first, but slowly you are able to straighten up. You emerge into a huge subterranean passage, that glows from an unseen source. The walls stretch- high above you, smooth in some places, in others rocky and hung with stalactites. Take the time to look around this place.

Short pause.

You notice there are painting materials lying on the floor of the cave. Someone has been here ahead of you - or perhaps some magic has brought these tools for you to use.. What happens now is up to you. These paints and brushes enable you to paint the inside of the cave, if you wish. Paint whatever comes to mind, and take your time.

Pause here for at least five minutes. I f you repeat this exercise you may like to give yourself longer periods to explore your images.

When you are ready, stand back to assess your work, or to assimilate any other experience you may have had. Now the walls of the cave dissolve around you, and you find yourself back in the outside world, at a cave mouth. Say a short prayer, give a 'thank you' or make a pledge - whatever you wish, to mark this experience.

Return in due time to everyday awareness. Write down what you have experienced. If this has been nothing, don't worry. Write down whatever you feel, for you may be surprised later at its significance, or a friend may notice a meaning that you have missed. Make yourself a drink and eat some fruit or a biscuit, to ensure that you are firmly back in th 'here and now'.

Chapter 6

Other Models

Say not 'I have found the truth' but rather, 'I have found a truth' Say not 'I have found the path of the soul'
Say rather, 'I have met the soul walking upon my path' For the soul walks upon all paths
The soul walks not upon a line, neither does it grow like a reed. The soul unfolds itself, like a lotus of countless petals

Kahlil Gibran, *The Prophet*

There are a number of masculine models that have been neglected in recent years. Let us now look at some of these

The Trickster
The elusive wisdom of the Trickster is not easily described. Truth has many faces and we all know we mustn't judge a book by its cover. With the Trickster we find that such trite sayings as 'Honesty is the best policy' and 'A thing worth doing is worth doing well' lose their value. We all know we lie at times - only a fool is always truthful, and a thing worth

doing is also worth doing badly. Some things are not come by on the straight and narrow. Janet and Stewart Farrar (see Further Reading) write:

> 'Unpredictability, contrary perhaps to popular belief, is a male-polarity aspect, one of the God functions. The Goddess and woman can be mysterious, but there is a subtle difference between unpredictability and mystery'.

Of course, this is not an invitation to do anything we fancy, whether we cause harm to others or not, and to follow the dictates of the ego. It is a reminder that rigid systems have their limits, that we need to adapt, and almost anything may be right, at certain times. Even the wise cannot be sure, and those who are sure are probably not wise.

Fionn Mac Cumhal

Fionn mac Cumhal appears in many Irish folk tales as a cunning hero with the gift of eternal life. Legend says that he built the causeway between Ireland and Scotland. He was the leader of the mighty Fianna - a band of warriors who defended Ireland long and valorously. Fionn never died, but rather wasted away into Otherworld, after the Fianna were slaughtered. Like King Arthur he sleeps, awaiting the time of his awakening.

One story about Fionn details how he stole the gift of knowledge from the poet Finegas. This poet had guarded the salmon of knowledge for seven years, knowing whoever ate of it would be all-wise. Fionn came to him in disguise, as his pupil, helped him to roast the salmon and sucked the hot juices off his thumb. Like the Arthurian Taliesin, who gains knowledge from the spilled drops from the cauldron of the goddess Cerridwen, Fionn thereby gains wisdom, except that, unlike Taliesin, his gift is no accident. Fionn knows what he is stealing. Why does he steal it, when, as a pupil, he might have come by it legitimately? Who can be sure - but that way he made sure he got it all, and quickly!

Loki

Norse legend tells of the infamous and wicked Loki. His worst and most notable deed involved the slaying of Baldur, the beautiful god of the Sun. Loki was one of the principal gods, the Aesir, and he was clever and seductive. Sometimes he could be co-operative and helpful, at others he was an underminer and a destroyer.

Baldur was handsome and well loved, and Loki is believed to have been jealous of him. He was son of Freya, the Nature goddess, and she had made all living things promise not to harm her darling son. All agreed readily, but Loki found out from her, by subtle questioning, that the mistletoe had been omitted, because it was too young. When all the gods were pelting invulnerable Baldur, for sport, Loki encouraged the blind god Hod to throw a mistletoe branch, and Baldur the Bright fell dead.

Desolated, the gods sent a messenger to the goddess Hel to ask her to return Baldur from the Underworld. She agreed, on one condition - that all living things should mourn him. Naturally everything agreed, for the Sun is loved by all. However, there was one exception - a certain ugly old giantess called Thokk, which turned out to be Loki in disguise. So Baldur had to remain in the Shadowland. Loki was discovered and chained to a rock by the Aesir, with a snake dripping venom upon his forehead. Some say he went mad, others that his faithful - and long-suffering - wife rescued him. Legend then tells how Loki joined the giants in their war on the gods and contributed to Ragnarok, the Twilight of the Gods, after which Baldur was one of those resurrected.

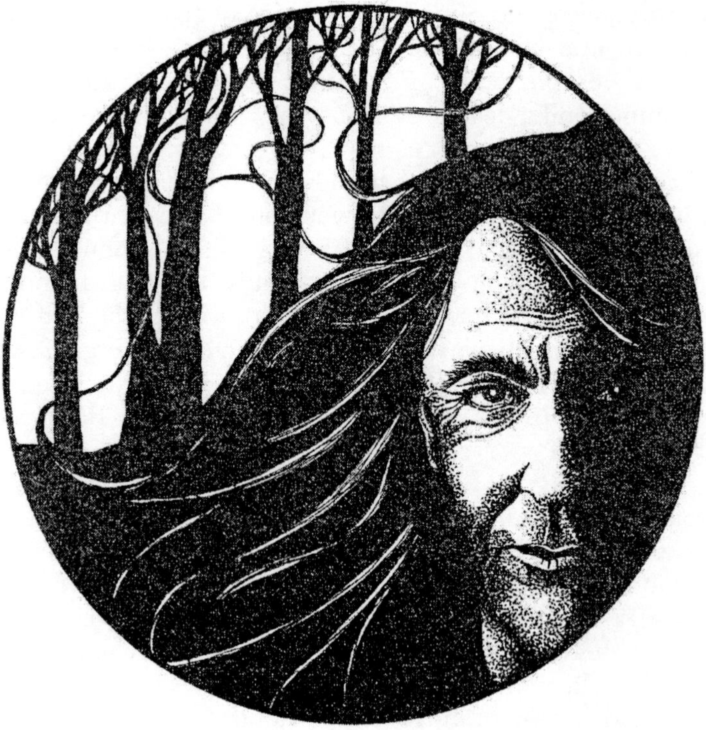

To us it seems that Baldur is one of many dying and resurrecting Sun gods, and the connection with the mistletoe, a feature of Yule when the Sun is 'reborn', lends weight to this. Loki, then, is the cruel but wise force that determines that light must be balanced by darkness, that death must take place as well as life - and here the Trickster has a part in fixing the seasonal cycle.

The Sacred Fool

Somewhat akin to the Trickster, the function of the Sacred Fool is to reveal viewpoints other than the obvious. Images in mythology are not clearly defined, but the Irish 'good god' the Daghda, springs to mind. The Daghda had a Cauldron of Abundance, and possessed a club that dealt death at one tip and gave life at the other. He it was who kept the golden harp of Ireland, and he was a great lord of magic. He is also represented as a figure of ribald fun, whose tunic did not cover his buttocks, and tales are told of his gluttony and sexual appetite.

The function of the Fool is to mock all that has been elevated by pomposity, preconception and prejudice. Alone in the medieval court, the Fool might poke fun at king and nobles with impunity, for at some level his function was recognised. One of our correspondents, a resident counsellor with a large company, recognises that to some extent his function is that of the Sacred Fool, where he can cast fresh light upon the institution he inhabits, but is not part of, and where he is able to show new perspectives on many situations and relationships. Perhaps a Fool should be employed specifically in all companies, in order that they keep their sense of values and humour!

The Magician

One of the best-known magicians is the Arthurian Merlin, who manipulates the royal bloodline to bring Uther and Ygraine together, so that Arthur may be conceived. Later he shows the boy where to find his authority in the Sword in the Stone, and he stands behind the throne with a depth of wisdom none can match.

As Magician, Merlin is aware of the cosmic web. He knows that Arthur's end is in his beginning, and he also knows, as Tolkien, the creator of the magician Gandalf writes, in Lord of the Rings, 'advice is a dangerous gift even from the wise to the wise'. Merlin also spends time in the wilderness, living as a Wild Man. He is aware of the energy undercurrents in all that takes place, and he lives with ambiguity - because of this he can see the invisible and is not always bound by ordinary laws, and he has power. He can manipulate the Unseen. Magicians are pictured as bringing about magical effects, but for these effects to take place the most major shifts are internal and these are huge. The Magician is a solitary figure, in touch with other dimensions. When we face contradiction and paradox, especially inside ourselves, when we undertake real inward transformation, then we are in the presence of the Magician, and we have 'power to'. As a wise magician, Merlin did not seek 'power over'.

The Lord of the Dance

> I danced in the morning when the world first began
> I danced in the moon and the stars and the sun
> I came down from heaven and I danced on earth
> In Bethlehem I had my birth ...
> They cut me down, but I leapt up high
> I am the light that will never, never die.
> And I'll live in you if you'll live in me
> I am the Lord of the Dance, said he.

We met the concept of 'dancing' in our chapter about the Hero, quoting the phrase 'Don't give a sword to a man who can't dance'. In the above-quoted hymn. Jesus Christ is 'Lord of the Dance' triumphing over death, generating endless joy and energy. In this he is one of the 'sacrificial' vegetation gods that is 'cut down' but rises again - proof of cycle, return, resurrection and eternity.

The hymn shows the exuberance of Jesus, champion of life, who has known death, and celebrates His gift - pleasure in living. Another Lord of the Dance is Shiva, the Hindu deity.

Shiva

Shiva is a rather ambivalent figure, for although his name means 'benevolent' he is also a personification of destructive forces. Shiva is often portrayed dancing, and his dance is the cycle of creation and destruction, of the total metabolism that is anabolism and katabolism.

He is Lord of the Dance of the Cosmos, and his terrible aspect is more in evidence than that of Christ. In the battle with the elemental forces, or demons, Shiva sent flame from his third eye and combined it with the anger of the gods - so bright was the conflagration that it blinded the gods and singed the beard of Brahma. Shiva does not destroy life, but he modifies it, and there are always balancing factors. He is an approachable god, who easily forgives supplicants.

In the Lord of the Dance we learn balance - for poise and balance are basic to all dancing. We also learn about the joy that is available to all those who surrender to the current of Life. Such is the joy of the ecstatic or mystic.

The Guardian

The motif of the Guardian is shown in many figures, such as the Nature deity, Cernunnos, and also generally in 'Father-God' shape. However, the true Guardian is not a patriarch. He does not 'guard' that which he regards as his, but he guards the inviolable, the mysterious. As guardians of England, Arthur and his knights are champions of the Earth, and the ideal is that they serve rather than possess. When Arthur is estranged from Guinevere, then the land suffers. Guinevere is not 'to blame' for her faithlessness, but rather the wastage occurs through lack of connection between masculine and feminine and especially loss of respect for the Feminine. This results in sterility at all levels. If Arthur is too immersed in the office of exalted kingship he cannot see the basic things that are before his eyes. He neglects relationships - and it is notable that Arthur and Guinevere have no child.

Arthur is Rex quondam, rexque futurus - the 'once and future king'. The heroic and magical age will dawn again when there is a true union between masculine and feminine, a proper and holy respect for the Earth and a sense of the masculine and feminine as balancing factors within each person. If we are inspired by the Guardian, that is our quest.

The Lover

We have seen in many stories how love has been a great inspiration to gods and heroes, Pan and Orpheus being but two. However, love in the sense of sheer physical passion is perhaps most colourfully embodied by female deities, such as Aphrodite. Perhaps we need to rediscover a figure of male passionate delight, similar to ecstatic Dionysus, only centred rather upon sexual love. Dionysus, in one tale of his birth, came from the mating of Zeus, father of the gods, with the Underworld queen, Persephone. At the time Zeus was in the shape of a snake - so this conception speaks of earthy, chthonic powers, and of resurrection, as the snake slithers into tombs, issues forth from its hole like a spring, and sloughs off its skin. Dionysus represented the removing of all inhibition, and his dancers, the maenads, were wild and ecstatic, sometimes even tearing people to pieces in their frenzy. Dionysus is a graphic reminder to respect the feral and the non-rational and to give them room. The legendary king Pentheus of Thebes tried to stop the riotous procession of the god's followers, and was torn to pieces for his pains. If we do not wish to share this fate, symbolically, then we have to 'forget ourselves' and let the Wild Man out at times. And the Wild Man can show the way to love, as in the case of Iron John.

To return to Zeus, another aspect reveals itself. Zeus was known as the great philanderer of Olympus, turning himself into all manner of shapes and animals in order to seduce his current amour. This does not seem very positive, for the 'Don Juan' approach is suggested, of someone who is unable to relate and who fears closeness on any deep level. However, what Zeus offered Olympus was integration. He called the counsels of the gods and goddesses and brought everyone together to make decisions. If we forget the possible tyrannical and patriarchal corruptions of this approach, there is that within the male psyche that often readily mobilises to integrate, focus and bring together. Unity is love. Integration promotes unity, and when brought about without repression or dictating it is a loving act.

Puer and Senex

These two terms derive from Jungian thought. The 'Puer Aeternus' is the Eternal Youth and the Senex is the Old Man. These figures turn up in various ways in myth and folklore, and often they struggle within the psyche of a man.

The 'puer' is a Peter Pan figure, who never grows old and never accepts the limitations of the flesh. Such statements as

'Hope I die before I get old', 'Live well, die young, be a beautiful corpse' and 'Eighteen till I die' are all 'puer' statements culled from popular music and film. The puer is very creative, but often his creations do not amount to as much as they could, for he is afraid to flesh them out. He is always flying above the ground - like Peter Pan - and he fears that his feet will bruise if he touches the earth. They will, and creations, when taken from the mind and translated to matter always disappoint, and the dream dies as the actuality - always a little inferior - is born. Some men are 'caught' in a puer stage. They cannot make relationships because that too pulls them down to earth. They fear they will lose something if they get grounded, and they are right. An exaggerated puer will literally prefer to die rather than age and may seem to seek death in extreme behaviour, such as racing driving (although by no means all racing drivers are puers). The puer fears the murky and the earthy, seeking the celestial realms - he likes to be 'above it all'. Robert Bly called all such types 'ascenders'. Naturally they have much to offer, but Peter Pan was wise when he sought his shadow and wanted Wendy to sew it back on for him. Only by making some true connection to the world and to real relationships can the puer achieve his promise.

The 'senex' is the other extreme. He is bound up in calcified structures even when young. He fears movement, life, lightness as forces that will deprive him of power as the puer fears stagnation, death and darkness as things that will limit him. The ancient Greek god, Cronos, swallowed all his children so they would not supplant him - in this way the senex fears the breath of the new. He suffocates, swallows, strangles and kills all that means growth, inspiration and - heaven help us! - change. Cronos has given us 'chronological', and the senex is conscious of time as a limiting factor. Indeed he is conscious of all limiting factors. The senex says 'Be careful', Watch your money', 'Don't take risks', 'Look before you leap', 'Best be on the safe side' and all the other little phrases that stop us in our tracks. The senex fears the fate of Cronos, whose son Zeus was concealed from him and later grew to be more powerful, so dethroning his father. The senex protects his power behind stone walls and engraves his laws on marble. His motto is 'If it moves, kill it'.

The senex isn't necessarily old, for he can be seen in many young men who cannot find joy in living and enter a dull nine-to-five at eighteen, without having explored their talents, who saddle themselves with mortgage and family 'because everyone does' and who rarely laugh. And the puer isn't necessarily young. Pickled puers can be found on stage and ski-slope, sporting wall-to-wall suntans and boasting so casually of their many conquests and ideas that you don't notice the tuft of grey hair that escaped the peroxide, or the little paunch above the designer jeans. The senex can be seen in many companies and in government, where all creativity is snuffed out before it reaches the top. The puer is seen in lots of imaginative schemes that remain castles in the air.

Naturally, the truth is that both puer and senex are needed, and each needs to respect the other and modify their approach. It is a good idea to ask ourselves whether we have become caught up in one of these archetypes, to the detriment of the totality of our self-expression. Can we recognise ourselves in either of these figures? If so, we need to seek - once again - that elusive state of balance. The image of the wise old man and the boy, meeting in dialogue, each having a love for the other, is an image of these two aspects coming together.

Practice You might find it revealing to think about the figures described in this chapter and where they may be needed in your life. Can you identify with the Lord of the Dance, or are you afraid to move? Are you able to fulfil the role of true Guardian when called upon, or do you fall into patterns of 'bossing'? What about the Lover? Is love a unifying factor for you, or another arena for competition and game playing? Can you play the Sacred Fool, or Trickster, willing to turn to new viewpoints, open to ideas, adaptable, and above all, able to laugh, especially at yourself? Or do you always walk straight ahead, with the vague feeling you are missing something? And what about the Magician, the most subtle figure. Are you seeking the magic of self-knowledge, or do you prefer to find ways to manipulate others? The models we have discussed show positive, inspiring ways to bring these dynamics into our

lives, but none of them should ever swamp us. No one is, or can aspire to be, Merlin, or Shiva, for they are beyond mortality. They are there for our inward awakening.

Chapter 7

Final Thoughts

There have been several themes for us to ponder, in previous chapters, regarding the potential of men, their present position and in what ways many seek to grow.

Balance

One of our contributors, Patrick Corbett, feels he can be helped by looking at male culture and heritage and how it might help him balance as a male. He is also aware of the value of meditations in this respect. Paul Duncan, another of our correspondents, writes: 'I believe we all should harmonise the male and female forces within ourselves and in the external world. A woman can find the Goddess within and hopefully now the man can express the God within.'

There is a growing awareness of the need for balance, as we have mentioned in earlier pages. Men realise that the pendulum has swung too far one way over the last 2,000 years. They are anxious to redress this, and to find that part of their inner selves which can understand and relate to the Feminine, as well as finding an identity of their own - perhaps this amounts to the same thing. From the yin/yang symbol we can see dark and light intertwined and see that each carries within it the seed of the other, like an eye. Perhaps without this balance, this piece of the 'other' within, we are blind.

Empathy

Empathy is often considered a feminine function, and men are conscious of needing to find this side of themselves, as we saw in Chapter 5. However, the Sumerian god Enki gives us a male model for empathy.

Inanna, Ereshkigal and Enki

Inanna, Queen of Heaven and Ereshkigal, Queen of the Underworld, are sisters, although estranged. Upon hearing of the death of Ereshkigal's husband, Inanna decides that she will go down to visit her grieving sister - her 'Underworld descent'. Inanna enters the infernal realms in all her regalia and Ereshkigal, already savage with grief, turns brutal and merciless. She strips Inanna of all her finery, kills her and hangs her on a meathook to rot - not a pretty picture!

In the upper world Inanna's absence is noticed and emissaries are dispatched to rescue the heavenly Queen - for how will creation continue without its brightest star? Ereshkigal is relentless, however, deaf to all pleas and lost in her own misery. What can be done?

It falls to Enki, the river god, to save the day. Enki was one of the creator deities, and the fish was his symbol. He instructed people in the arts of handicrafts, farming, writing, laws, building and magic, and when his teaching was complete he returned to the sea. Legend told how he lived with the earth mother, Ninhursag, on a paradisiacal island. Now, when approached for help, he has no doubt what to do. Taking the good dirt from under his fingernails he fashions little mourners that go to Ereshkigal and commiserate. They do not try to cheer her up or persuade her to do anything - they just empathise. At length, feeling her loneliness eased, Ereshkigal brightens. She releases Inanna, who comes back to life - as goddesses are wont to do - and returns to the daylight and her throne in heaven. Gods and humans now rejoice!

Commentary

We see here that Enki has acted as the first therapist. He realises the simple value of empathy. Note that he is a river god - water is an element often associated with the Feminine, and with feeling, but Enki is male. Also he looks to the dirt beneath his nails for the means to comfort. He looks to the despised or ignored. He uses the earth that has gathered there - he goes back to basics and he turns filth to creativity. Every therapist knows that in the murkiest depths of the personality lie the greatest treasures and the best potential for creative change. Enki is dynamic - he does something with what he finds, not intrusively but effectively. He is a role model for empathy in the male.

Initiation

We have touched on the theme of initiation in earlier pages. For modem men this 'ritual' is largely absent. Smoking behind the bike-shed, taking drugs, communal masturbation and first sex may take the place of true initiation, but they are poor and fumbling substitutes. The simple fact seems to be that there are no real modes of initiation for young males in our society. The advent of menstruation initiates women. Their monthly cycle connects them to all cycles in Earth and cosmos, and brings the reality of life and death, endings and beginnings in a vivid body-knowledge. Although this is insufficiently valued, at least it is there. For men there is nothing corresponding.

Many young men do seek to be initiated. They enter tennis or football clubs and hang around older men, hoping, unconsciously, to be shown something. The less fortunate or less aware band into groups and raise hell, searching for something of value, something that can soothe, calm, make whole. They are far more likely to find time in a prison cell and a life of frustration and growing violence. Of course, there is more at work here than the need for initiation. However, there is a tragic lack of knowledge about what it is to be a man and how to get there.

In *Iron John* Robert Bly speaks of some rather barbaric practices where 'holy terror' is caused to enter boys. From some frightening ordeals, which bring home to boys the value of life and its dangers and pains, they come to understand male comfort and closeness, true depth of experience and responsibility. We do doubt this approach somewhat. Many writers contend that male initiations often ape menstruation. Surely it is unnecessary to inflict cruelty. Surely men can find something of their own. some meaning to masculinity that older men can mediate to boys?

We feel this is an area for exploration. Simply, we would suggest that some challenging activity be undertaken in company with older men. where the boy can learn to push himself to the limit, to rely on himself, but also to see from being with someone more experienced that this is something men can undertake. Depending on the boy, this might be physical or mental, but probably it needs to be challenging - there seems to be something within the male psyche that seeks this. A boy needs to be brought into vibrant, blinding contact with the essence and meaning of the life-death cycle and his place therein. This does not necessarily need to be spelt out, for often matters are more effectual at an instinctive level. One way to this could be by vision-quest. Older, wiser men may be able to discern what is suitable for an individual boy - however, there may at present be a dearth of these older, wiser men! This is an avenue that needs to be developed by the men of the twenty-first century.

The Father

Since the Industrial Revolution fathers have been separated for much of the working day from their sons and daughters. Because of this it is not possible to learn from the actual physical presence of the father. This leaves a gap, and into this gap washes a tide of doubt, suspicion and unrecognised longing. This is a matter explored at length by Robert Bly. We would simply say what every psychologist and soap opera seems to be saying - fathers need to be with their children. Sons and daughters both suffer from the 'absent father' but for the boy there are special problems, for where can he learn about manhood if not from his father? 'Quality time' is not enough. Where possible children need to go into their father's place of work. Hours spent mending bikes and doing shopping together are better than one hour of 'special attention'. Children are often bewildered and frustrated by adults giving them special attention - apart, of course, from those times when we all know extra support is needed. Children want to know how to become adults - playing with them isn't enough. Sons need to be taken into the world of the father. If sons cannot be taken to work, perhaps they can be involved in outings with work colleagues, or shared activities, sports, projects and such like.

One of the greatest shifts in consciousness in the twentieth century has come from the development of depth psychology, yet while modern science and business studies are taught in schools, this aspect is neglected. Despite send-ups and cliches, there seems little doubt that most psychological problems stem from infancy - is it not worthwhile teaching youngsters as much as possible about these concepts, so improving their chance of being reasonable parents? Of course, not much can be taken in at a purely intellectual level, but it is worth considering.

Water Jar Boy

This native American tale tells of the boy's search for his father.

One day a girl was making jars. As she smoothed the clay, a little water got up inside her. To her surprise she became pregnant, and when the baby was born it was a little jar!

The small jar was fed through the neck, and it grew quickly. Soon it asked to go hunting with the grandfather, who reluctantly agreed. During the hunt the jar broke, and when the grandfather went looking for the jar he was incredulous to see a boy appear.

Now the boy had a yearning to find his father, but everyone said this was impossible. However, the boy set off up-river to the spring. When he arrived at the spring, a man was there waiting for him. At first the man seemed frightening but the boy held his ground. 'I am sure you are my father,' he said. 'Yes, I am your father,' admitted the man at length, and held out his arms. He showed his son a new country beside the spring and all the people came out to welcome the boy as their kin.

The boy went home to tell his mother that he had found his father, but she became ill and died. 'Now there is nothing more for me here,' said the boy. Back to the spring he went, to find his father, and there he found his mother also living. His father was Red Water Snake, a powerful totem. Now they all might live together.

Commentary

This myth speaks of the essential mystery of male parentage. No one can be quite sure, except the mother, who is the father of a child - but there is more to it than this. We have basic knowledge of our mothers, because we grew in the womb for nine months. Of our fathers there was only a tiny seed, back at the beginning. So we may be conscious of a need to reconnect, but this may not be easy.

The boy is in a 'jar'. He is encased in something misleading, but when this shell of misconception and misperception cracks, he realises that he needs to find his father.

At first the father does not welcome him, fathers are not quite as soft and accepting as mothers. Their love is one of testing in order that we become prepared for life. However, the father loves him - he has been looking for him all the time.

Truly 'finding' the father means the old perception of the mother 'dies'. However, what is made possible is greater unity between the masculine and the feminine. Having found his father and thereby his way to manhood, the boy can now see his parents as a couple - and so find the way to inner balance, and possibly to being part of a 'couple' himself at some future time.

Native American stories have immense subtlety and breadth which we have no doubt hardly touched. Father as a Red Water Snake symbolises life at its most profound.

Role Models

Graham Boston has this to say on the subject: '... there are a lack of male role models in society due to confusion about what is good and bad about our natures ... what is needed is democratic discussion and debate about values, and about what kind of society we would like to see for ourselves and future generations.'

An idea important to Howard is that 'We are the forefathers of the future'. This is a fact we need to bear in mind, and it can give a sense of responsibility about coming generations that may be lost in despair and confusion. It is hard for men thrust into public life, perhaps as actors or sports personalities, to bear in mind their role-model status - especially as they may be confused themselves. However, the old values and religious dogmas are being questioned and discarded. Until something new and reasonably clear evolves, young men are bound to turn to such for guidance. This fact may need to be addressed. General, social and spiritual role models are required, although the age of leaders and gurus is passing. Each person must become his or her own spiritual authority. In this, attitude and guidance are important, for dogma is no longer acceptable. We come back to the importance of the personal father as a caring, helping, supporting, testing and guiding factor.

Belief Systems

The demise of the traditional models, 'family values', discipline and the work ethic are certainly leaving a vacuum. In a society where old ladies are bound, gagged, beaten and robbed in their homes and teachers are in physical danger in the classroom, loud voices are calling to bring back the 'old values'. The true 'value' and meaning of traditional systems is not always examined, nor is the wider context taken. Is not the very gung-ho attitude that creates our current problems the same as the approach of the offenders? 'Birch them', 'lock them up and throw away the key', 'hang them' are parents to 'mug him and steal his wallet', 'rape her', 'kill him', 'break down the door and take what you want'. As Amnesty

International can verify, countries where state penalties are the most cruel are those where there is greatest civilian violence - state-sanctioned brutality has been shown to give rise to crimes, not to prevent them.

In contrast, what is sometimes disparagingly called the 'do-gooder approach' sends persistent young offenders on expensive holidays and provides convicted paedophiles with outings to the zoo. Neither of these approaches seem to have the answer - and no one can possibly have 'the answer' as such. Our suggestions are to foster respect - something which a friend of ours recently identified as the most important thing in relationships. It's no good talking to young people about respecting their elders, if their elders patently respect little but profit and money and have no respect for the ecosystem.

Pagan values emphasise community, celebration and identification with the rhythms of Nature. No catechisms are required and there are no laws except 'Harm none'. Most of the figures described in this book are 'pagan'. Essentially this is about realising that we are all part of something greater - doing and feeling, not just believing and obeying, and developing an inner relationship with the Divine. Respect for the environment as the embodiment of God and Goddess are also pivotal to pagans. Paganism, by its approach of acceptance, certainly offers a pathway where fear is minimised, both of hidden aspects of ourselves and of what life may have in store. We think it is worth a try!

Joblessness

This is such an issue for many men that is needs addressing as a priority. Political comments are outside our scope. We merely stress the need to provide men, young and old, with practical and spiritual resources to cope with the fact they do not always have something useful to do. Men need to feel they have status and value if they are not able to find work. Time without a job can be treasured as an opportunity, say, for vision quest. Only by men getting together and offering each other support can men begin to feel 'okay' about not having a job to go to. Women have, at times, the possibly doubtful recourse of having a baby. For men there is nothing similar. However, there are so many valuable things one might do with one's time off that a great asset may be left unexploited because jobless men feel too ashamed or despondent (or resentful) to make use of it.

Being a Partner

Many men are asking themselves how to fulfil the role of partner to a woman. Feeling they are expected to be both strong and sensitive, neither masterful nor a 'wimp', men often feel uncertain. This uncertainty is increased because men tend to feel they should be decisive, but are unable to discuss the issue sensibly with other men. The question of 'how to handle a woman' is regarded as a matter of mystery, requiring special techniques, and has been made the subject of a popular song - perhaps to contain men's anxiety.

The answer is at once simple but also quite difficult. What most women want is a man who is adult, who has the courage to face his vulnerability and explore his inner conflicts. Many women find themselves in a position where they are coping with the unacknowledged insecurities of their mate, and this is a thankless task that often means they get the blame. A simple example is that of the man who is irrationally jealous, and who is unwilling or unable to explore the reasons for his jealousy - so his partner may have to cope with accusations, and even violence. A more complex scenario is that of the man who knows his jealousy is irrational, but refuses to work with it, expecting his partner to avoid giving him the smallest cause for unease. Many situations are much more subtle and complex.

As we explored in Chapter 4, a modern hero is one who has the courage to face his internal demons and to take responsibility for his actions, feelings and responses. That is much more important than who opens the door for whom.

The Future

The present system will not die overnight, but if enough men are calling for change, as women have been doing for a long time, then change will come about. The upward-thrusting, building and galvanising spirit of the masculine is invaluable. It is this spirit that has brought us into the Space Age, and if it can be combined with and modified by gentler and more holistic attitudes, there is hope for the birth of a new consciousness and a clearer recognition of our place in the cosmos. Let us end with these words of Graham Boston:

> *For me I cannot see the world as composed of men on the one hand and women on the other. When I see the world as composed of PEOPLE - individuals who are unique yet bound by common humanity, I see a much broader, more inspiring ... picture.*

Practice

You may like to consider the question of initiation. Do you feel you have been 'initiated'? What did this entail? Or if you feel initiation has been absent, what would you like to experience? What forms could be found for this process? What ideas do you have? How would you, as a grown man, try to initiate a boy?

What do you think about role models? Do you/did you have any?

As a role model, what would you seek to provide for others?

What about your relationship with your father? Has this been adequate?

What would you have liked to receive that you did not get? And how would you seek to provide this for your own children, or those under your guidance?

Further Reading and Resources

Further Reading

Wheel of the Year - Myth and Magic Through the Seasons: Teresa Moorey and Jane Brideson: Capall Bann 2003
Looking at the many meanings of the seasonal cycle, with myths, activities and meditation.

Fire In The Belly - On Being A Man; Sam Keen, Piatkus, 1992
This is a valuable work for addressing male gender issues squarely and honestly. There is much practical and inspiring material here, and male roles are re-examined and re-evaluated in a modern context.

He; Robert Johnson
Using myth, the author reveals much about the male psyche. A great aid to understanding.

His Story - Masculinity in the Post-Patriarchal World; Nicholas Mann, Llewellyn, 1995
A frank, imaginative and radical examination of masculinity, looking for ways to reclaim the sacred, to relate, to uncover the meaning of lost traditions and discover a source of power. Recommended.

Iron John; Robert Bly, Element, 1993
Reassessing men's position and using the tale of Iron john as a symbolic and poetic medium to convey ideas. Inspiring for men - possibly does not address feminist issues sufficiently or fairly.

The Witches' God; Janet and Stewart Farrar, Phoenix, 1989.
A clear and interesting look at the pagan God in many forms. Rituals are suggested, and a hundred-page glossary of the gods of the world is included. A useful book.

Resources

Shamanic contacts e.g. for Vision Quest (N.B. Enclose SAE.)

Faculty of Shamanics, Kenneth Meadows, PO Box 300, Potters Bar, Herts, EN6 4LE, UK.

Eagles Wing, Leo Rutherford, 58 Westbere Road, NW2 3RU, UK.

Different Drum, 71 Painswick Road, Cheltenham, Glos, GL50 2EX, UK.

Music - Lyrics quoted at chapter headings.

Seventh Wave Music, PO Box 1, Totnes, Devon, TQ9 6UQ UK. Music inspired by ancient pagan roots - catalogue available.

Joining A Men's Group
Look in alternative therapy centres, alternative bookshops, or similar, for advertisements regarding local men's groups. If you cannot find one then you could advertise in similar places to start your own.

Always be very careful when starting or joining a group. Occasionally inexperienced seekers have been known to be exploited, sexually and otherwise, by the unscrupulous. Steer well clear of anyone who seems at all suspect or who promises short cuts to initiation or enlightenment. No one who is sincere will ever expect you to do anything you feel in any way uncomfortable about. Keep your self-respect and your commonsense at all times.

Pagan Federation, BM Box 7097 London WC 1 N 3XX

Thunder Road - a nine-month educational programme to inspire, motivate and provide moral and spiritual guidance to young men; an idea born from the men's movement. For further information contact Michael Boyle. Tel: 01202 757522.

Children of Artemis   www.witchcraft.org

Canada
The Minstrel (pagan magazine) PO Box 3068, Winnipeg, MB R3C 4E5.

United States
Green Egg (eco-pagan magazine) Box 1542, Ukiah, CA 95482.

Circle Network News (pagan newspaper) PO Box 219, Mt Horeb, WI 53572.

Australia
Pan Pacific Pagan Alliance, PO Box 1, Perthville, NSW 2795.

Church Of All Worlds, PO Box 408, Woden, ACT 2606.

N.B: Always enclose a stamped, self-addressed envelope or international reply coupons. Magazines will have lists of further contacts.

To contact the Author:-

undines@btopenworld.co.uk
www.westwitch.net

FREE DETAILED CATALOGUE

Capall Bann is owned and run by people actively involved in many of the areas in which we publish. A detailed illustrated catalogue is available on request, SAE or International Postal Coupon appreciated. **Titles can be ordered direct from Capall Bann, post free in the UK** (cheque or PO with order) or from good bookshops and specialist outlets.

Angels and Goddesses - Celtic Christianity & Paganism, M. Howard
Arthur - The Legend Unveiled, C Johnson & E Lung
Astrology The Inner Eye - A Guide in Everyday Language, E Smith
Auguries and Omens - The Magical Lore of Birds, Yvonne Aburrow
Asyniur - Womens Mysteries in the Northern Tradition, S McGrath
Beginnings - Geomancy, Builder's Rites & Electional Astrology in the European Tradition, Nigel Pennick
Between Earth and Sky, Julia Day
Book of the Veil , Peter Paddon
Caer Sidhe - Celtic Astrology and Astronomy, Michael Bayley
Call of the Horned Piper, Nigel Jackson
Cat's Company, Ann Walker
Celtic Faery Shamanism, Catrin James
Celtic Lore & Druidic Ritual, Rhiannon Ryall
Celtic Sacrifice - Pre Christian Ritual & Religion, Marion Pearce
Celtic Saints and the Glastonbury Zodiac, Mary Caine
Circle and the Square, Jack Gale
Compleat Vampyre - The Vampyre Shaman, Nigel Jackson
Creating Form From the Mist - The Wisdom of Women in Celtic Myth and Culture, Lynne Sinclair-Wood
Crystal Clear - A Guide to Quartz Crystal, Jennifer Dent
Crystal Doorways, Simon & Sue Lilly
Crossing the Borderlines - Guising, Masking & Ritual Animal Disguise in the European Tradition, Nigel Pennick
Dragons of the West, Nigel Pennick
Earth Dance - A Year of Pagan Rituals, Jan Brodie
Earth Harmony - Places of Power, Holiness & Healing, Nigel Pennick
Earth Magic, Margaret McArthur
Eildon Tree (The) Romany Language & Lore, Michael Hoadley
Enchanted Forest - The Magical Lore of Trees, Yvonne Aburrow
Eternal Priestess, Sage Weston
Eternally Yours Faithfully, Roy Radford & Evelyn Gregory

Everything You Always Wanted To Know About Your Body, But So Far Nobody's Been Able To Tell You, Chris Thomas & D Baker
Face of the Deep - Healing Body & Soul, Penny Allen
Fairies in the Irish Tradition, Molly Gowen
Familiars - Animal Powers of Britain, Anna Franklin
Forest Paths - Tree Divination, Brian Harrison, Ill. S. Rouse
From Past to Future Life, Dr Roger Webber
God Year, The, Nigel Pennick & Helen Field
Goddess on the Cross, Dr George Young
Goddess Year, The, Nigel Pennick & Helen Field
Goddesses, Guardians & Groves, Jack Gale
Handbook For Pagan Healers, Liz Joan
Handbook of Fairies, Ronan Coghlan
Healing Book, The, Chris Thomas and Diane Baker
Healing Homes, Jennifer Dent
Healing Stones, Sue Philips
Herb Craft - Shamanic & Ritual Use of Herbs, Lavender & Franklin
In Search of Herne the Hunter, Eric Fitch
Inner Celtia, Alan Richardson & David Annwn
Inner Mysteries of the Goths, Nigel Pennick
Intuitive Journey, Ann Walker Isis - African Queen, Akkadia Ford
Journey Home, The, Chris Thomas
Legend of Robin Hood, The, Richard Rutherford-Moore
Lid Off the Cauldron, Patricia Crowther
Light From the Shadows - Modern Traditional Witchcraft, Gwyn
Lore of the Sacred Horse, Marion Davies
Lost Lands & Sunken Cities (2nd ed.), Nigel Pennick
Magic of Herbs - A Complete Home Herbal, Rhiannon Ryall
Magical Guardians - Exploring the Spirit and Nature of Trees, Philip Heselton
Magical History of the Horse, Janet Farrar & Virginia Russell
Magical Lore of Animals, Yvonne Aburrow
Magical Lore of Cats, Marion Davies
Magical Lore of Herbs, Marion Davies
Magick Without Peers, Ariadne Rainbird & David Rankine
Masks of Misrule - Horned God & His Cult in Europe, Nigel Jackson
Mind Massage - 60 Creative Visualisations, Marlene Maundrill
Mirrors of Magic - Evoking the Spirit of the Dewponds, P Heselton
Moon Mysteries, Jan Brodie
Mysteries of the Runes, Michael Howard
Mystic Life of Animals, Ann Walker
New Celtic Oracle The, Nigel Pennick & Nigel Jackson
Pagan Feasts - Seasonal Food for the 8 Festivals, Franklin & Phillips
Patchwork of Magic - Living in a Pagan World, Julia Day
Pathworking - A Practical Book of Guided Meditations, Pete Jennings
Personal Power, Anna Franklin
Pickingill Papers - The Origins of Gardnerian Wicca, Bill Liddell

Pillars of Tubal Cain, Nigel Jackson
Places of Pilgrimage and Healing, Adrian Cooper
Practical Meditation, Steve Hounsome
Psychic Self Defence - Real Solutions, Jan Brodie
Real Fairies, David Tame
Romany Tapestry, Michael Houghton
Sacred Animals, Gordon MacLellan
Sacred Celtic Animals, Marion Davies, Ill. Simon Rouse
Sacred Dorset - On the Path of the Dragon, Peter Knight
Sacred Grove - The Mysteries of the Forest, Yvonne Aburrow
Sacred Geometry, Nigel Pennick
Sacred Ring - Pagan Origins of British Folk Festivals, M. Howard
Season of Sorcery - On Becoming a Wisewoman, Poppy Palin
Seasonal Magic - Diary of a Village Witch, Paddy Slade
Secret Places of the Goddess, Philip Heselton
Secret Signs & Sigils, Nigel Pennick
Spirits of the Earth series, Jaq D Hawkins
Stony Gaze, Investigating Celtic Heads John Billingsley
Stumbling Through the Undergrowth, Mark Kirwan-Heyhoe
Subterranean Kingdom, The, revised 2nd ed, Nigel Pennick
Symbols of Ancient Gods, Rhiannon Ryall
Talking to the Earth, Gordon MacLellan
Taming the Wolf - Full Moon Meditations, Steve Hounsome
Teachings of the Wisewomen, Rhiannon Ryall
The Other Kingdoms Speak, Helena Hawley
Tree: Essence of Healing, Simon & Sue Lilly
Understanding Chaos Magic, Jaq D Hawkins
Warp and Weft - In Search of the I-Ching, William de Fancourt
Warriors at the Edge of Time, Jan Fry
Water Witches, Tony Steele
Way of the Magus, Michael Howard
Weaving a Web of Magic, Rhiannon Ryall
West Country Wicca, Rhiannon Ryall
Wildwitch - The Craft of the Natural Psychic, Poppy Palin
Wildwood King, Philip Kane
Working With the Merlin, Geoff Hughes

FREE detailed catalogue and FREE 'Inspiration' magazine

Contact Capall Bann Publishing, Auton Farm, Milverton, Somerset, TA4 1NE